Latin American Land Reforms
in Theory and Practice

To David Stanfield

Thanks for all your help.

Peter Dorner

Latin American
Land Reforms
in Theory and Practice

A Retrospective Analysis

The University of Wisconsin Press

The University of Wisconsin Press
114 North Murray Street
Madison, Wisconsin 53715

3 Henrietta Street
London WC2E 8LU, England

Printed in the United States of America

Library of Congress Cataloging-in-Publication Data
Dorner, Peter, 1925–
    Latin American land reforms in theory and practice:
a retrospective analysis / Peter Dorner.
    120 pp.   cm.
    Includes bibliographical references and index.
    ISBN 0-299-13160-2   ISBN 0-299-13164-5 (pbk.)
    1. Land reform—Latin America. I. Title.
    HD1333.L29D67   1991
333.3'18—dc20   91-26440

Contents

Tables

Preface

This monograph deals with the political, social, economic, and institutional aspects and the outcomes of land reforms attempted in Latin America over the past thirty years. Its purpose is to summarize and synthesize the ongoing debate about land reform. It deals with competing theoretical and ideological positions and draws policy conclusions from reform experiences. Reforms are analyzed in light of corollary changes in agricultural and industrial systems and population dynamics. The last chapter comments briefly on the role that international agencies can play in the sensitive national policy decisions that are at the heart of any serious attempts at land reform.

This analysis necessarily includes criticism of some key actors and actions. At times I take issue with professional analysts, foreign assistance administrators, and national politicians and critique specific policies. However, I do not intend to belittle the ideas of others or to denigrate the policies of Latin American governments. Every nation, including the United States, has its share of unresolved social and economic problems. Restructuring land tenure institutions through land reform is an exceedingly difficult political undertaking. I have enduring respect for those who have had the courage to try it.

In preparing this manuscript, I have been most fortunate in having excellent research assistance from Teen K. Barua and Cynthia Williams. The outstanding editorial and production assistance received from Jane Dennis and John Bielefeldt are gratefully acknowledged. Finally, I am indebted to my colleagues who read early drafts and provided most helpful comments and suggestions—Marion Brown, John Bruce, Michael Carter, Don Kanel, David Stanfield, and William Thiesenhusen. I appreciate especially the encouragement given by Marion Brown, who is responsible for my undertaking this project and whose excellent comments and suggestions were indispensable to the completion of this manuscript. At the same time, all of the above are absolved of any responsibility for things said or left unsaid. This responsibility is mine alone. I am grateful for the financial assistance received from the Agency for International Development and from the University of Wisconsin–Madison. Like my colleagues, these institutions bear no responsibility for any of the ideas expressed in this manuscript.

Latin American Land Reforms in Theory and Practice

1

The Politics of Reform

Land Reform as a Political Issue

Latin American agriculture, with few exceptions, is characterized by a high concentration of landownership. In recent decades large numbers of rural people have migrated to the cities. The agricultural sector has a great potential for increasing output and for employing more people. Concentrated landownership accompanies a highly skewed distribution of income. These conditions lead to recurring and sometimes violent demands for land redistribution and reform.

The salient reform issue in Latin America and elsewhere is and has always been redistribution of agricultural lands. In many countries, inequities associated with land tenure have been ignored until oppressed rural people rebelled. Feudal land tenure systems and the struggle of peasants for rights to land were key factors in the French Revolution. The American Civil War was a conflict over land as well as a struggle over slavery (Conrad and Meyer 1964). The Homestead Act of 1862, which provided full title to 160 acres of public land after five years of residence and evidence of improvements, was passed only after many years of debate. The southern states were threatened by a free land policy because it undermined the slave system, which was the foundation for cotton production on plantations in the south. There were not enough votes in both houses of Congress to pass the Homestead Act until the southern states seceded over the slavery issue (Edwards 1940; Dorner 1979). The failure to follow through with a land reform after the Civil War has cast a century-long shadow over race relations and the economic opportunities of Afro-Americans. The slaves were free, but they did not have the independent economic opportunities that could have been theirs had a land reform been carried out. (See also Geisler and Popper 1984; Dorner 1986.)

The twentieth-century revolutions in Mexico and Bolivia were fueled by major injustices in landholding patterns. The overthrow of Batista in Cuba and Somoza in Nicaragua, as well as the current civil war in El Salvador and the continuing turmoil in the Philippines, all have their origins in land tenure institutions that favor a small group of wealthy families at the expense of millions of impoverished rural people.

3

Glaring as these inequities may become, they are not easily remedied. Any reform worthy of the name is a very difficult political undertaking. It involves a realignment of economic and political power. While it may not be entirely a zero-sum game, some groups certainly lose while others gain. Galbraith's (1951) succinct analysis of nearly four decades ago still holds true:

> Unfortunately some of our current discussion of land reform in the undeveloped countries proceeds as though this reform were something that a government proclaims on any fine morning—that it gives land to the tenants as it might give pensions to old soldiers or as it might reform the administration of justice. In fact, a land reform is a revolutionary step; it passes power, property, and status from one group in the community to another. If the government of the country is dominated or strongly influenced by the landholding group— the one that is losing its prerogatives—no one should expect effective land legislation as an act of grace. . . . The world is composed of many different kinds of people, but those who own land are not so different—whether they live in China, Persia, Mississippi, or Quebec—that they will meet and happily vote themselves out of its possession. (695–96)

The Peasants' Role in the Evolution of Political Systems

As Galbraith says, no landed class ever voted itself out of its privileged position. But neither has the peasantry of the world been entirely docile and acceptant of its landless status. At the core of the agrarian question is a strong desire and an urgently felt need among rural people for the security inherent in owning a plot of land. Rural problems are not instigated or created by political activists from outside. Peasants invariably and persistently demand measures to break the land monopoly that keeps property in the hands of an elite which dominates political and economic life. It is this legacy, and not necessarily left-wing extremism (though this can certainly be an added force), that is the root cause of the internal unrest in rural areas in many Third World nations.

The distribution of landownership is often a key factor in determining the direction of a transition from one form of social and political order to another. The transformation of an agrarian system into an industrial economy requires vast changes in many institutions, including those of land tenure. Barrington Moore (1966) suggests that the nature of the sociopolitical-economic system resulting from this transformation reflects the underlying and preexisting agrarian structures and the role of peasants in changing them. He concludes that a common experience in all industrializing countries has been that of separating a substantial segment of the ruling classes from direct ties to the land. Skocpol (1982) points out that before Moore's book was published,

> the peasant, especially, was spurned as the repository of conservatism and tradition, of all that needed to be overcome by a revolutionary bourgeoisie or proletariat or by a modernizing elite. But once the United States became tragically engaged from the mid-1960s in a military effort to halt the Vietnamese Revolution, U.S. scholars quite understandably became fascinated with the revolutionary potential of the peasantry—especially in the Third World. (351–52)

Huntington (1968) argues that a broadening political consciousness in many Third World countries puts the countryside at center stage as the main source of stability or instability for a political system or government. "Modernization" has produced a worsening of the real conditions of peasants' work and welfare. In turn, their aspirations for a better life have grown stronger. As the barriers of communication between the countryside and the city have broken down, the peasantry has come in contact with urban intellectuals who may espouse revolutionary ideas. The peasants come to realize not only that they are suffering but also that something can be done about it.

The peasants' wants and demands may often conflict with those of the intelligentsia, but the revolutionary intellectuals are ready to support the peasants. "Efforts by intellectuals to arouse peasants almost invariably fail unless the social and economic conditions of the peasantry are such as to give them concrete motives for revolt," says Huntington (1968, 303). "The intelligentsia can ally themselves with a revolutionary peasantry, but they cannot create a revolutionary peasantry." Huntington concludes that if the countryside supports the political system and the government,

> the system itself is secure against revolution, and the government has some hope of making itself secure against rebellion. If the countryside is in opposition, both system and government are in danger of overthrow. The role of the countryside is variable: it is either the source of stability or the source of revolution. (292)

In other words, "If no government can come to power which can win the support or the acquiescence of the countryside, then little basis exists for political stability" (291–92).

Prosterman et al. (1981) agree that

> landless peasants have provided the rank and file support for most of the great twentieth-century revolutions—those, in particular, of Mexico, Russia, China, and Vietnam. They have played a similar role in many lesser bloodlettings, such as the revolutions in Cuba, Ethiopia, and Bolivia, and the

failed insurgencies in Kenya, Malaysia, and the Philippines. The problems of landlessness are heavily implicated in many other episodes of upheaval and civil strife, ranging from the civil war in Spain to the overthrow of the Shah in Iran. (53–54)

In the Philippines, the Huk insurgency of the early 1950s was put down with the help of the United States, and land reform was avoided (see, for example, Shalom 1977). Yet it is evident today that the supposedly successful anti-Huk campaign was not a solution at all; the radical New People's Army is taking land by force and threatens Philippine society more than ever. Its support base, as it was for the Huks, is the peasantry, whose grievances are mostly land-related.

Asian Reforms and the U.S. Role

In the decade following World War II, the United States was deeply involved in sweeping agrarian reforms in Japan, Taiwan, and South Korea. Some relatively ideal conditions for land reform existed in these countries. In Japan, the U.S. occupation was the governmental force firmly committed to reform. In Taiwan, the exiled government from the mainland, having seen the consequences of an alienated peasantry and lacking a major stake in landownership in Taiwan, was anxious to win the support of the tenant farmers. In South Korea, the U.S. influence was also very significant.

Although they have had much impact on U.S. thinking about land reform, the transformations of the agrarian structures in Japan, Taiwan, and South Korea were unique in many ways and did not warrant the expectation that the same formula could be exported to other countries. In addition to the unique political power arrangements suggested above, there were many other features favorable to these reforms. First of all, the prereform land-tenure system in these countries can best be characterized as a structure of small operatorship, tenancy units. The main target of these reforms was the irrigated rice lands, and there were long traditions of farmer organizations. These organizations were strengthened by the reforms and played a key role in the transition and in helping to serve the reform's beneficiaries. The reforms basically consisted of cutting the tie between tenants and their landlords—abolishing the rent collection and control system. These tenants already had a long tradition of relatively independent entrepreneurial activity (see Kikuchi and Hayami 1978; Hayami and Ruttan 1971.)

Thus there was a long tradition of intensive agriculture on small operating units (tenant farms). By the late 1940s to the early 1950s, commercial fertilizers, improved varieties, and other scientific practices were well established. The additional postreform incentives created for tenant producers by freeing them from rents (as well as a strong demand and, slightly later, a favorable cost/price ratio) resulted in a very progressive agriculture. Clearly not all of these results were attributable to the reform, but its impact was undeniable. However, the assumption that similar results would be forthcoming from Latin American reforms was not warranted. The Asian unimodal system stood in sharp contrast to the dualistic farm-size structure prevailing in most of Latin America.

Land Reform and the U.S. Policy Dilemma

As noted earlier, redistributive land reforms are inherently difficult political undertakings because they affect directly the alignments of economic and political power within a nation. However, this very realignment, when and where it has occurred in Latin America, has brought political conflicts within the United States as well.

The contrast between some of the homegrown reforms in Latin America and the U.S.-led Asian reforms is again striking. As shown above, the Asian system of tenure consisted of concentrated ownership but decentralized small-farm *operatorship*. In much of Latin America, large *operating* units must be dealt with in reforms. Because of capital infrastructures and underdeveloped entrepreneurial skills among the potential beneficiaries, redistributive land reforms in Latin America have frequently set up some type of communal or collective arrangement; the establishment of small, independent operating units would have been, at least initially, much more costly. In the Asian reforms the resulting family-farm *owner-operator* systems and the apparent reliance on market mechanisms was wholly consistent with U.S. experience and ideology.

These were not the only differences. In the late 1940s and early 1950s, there were few U.S. private interests (multinational corporations) in Asia. This was not the case with Cuba and the rest of Latin America in the late 1950s and 1960s. Despite the anticommunist fears that some sought to exploit in the United States at that time, the U.S. was unchallenged in its economic, industrial, technological, and military dominance. The ubiquitous metric of judging U.S. reponses to Third World issues in terms of superpower conflicts was not so prevalent in the early 1950s. Beginning with Cuba, a major dilemma has been that any Latin American government radical and strong enough to carry through a redistributive land reform inevitably came into conflict with the ideological stance of the U.S. government. Following Cuba, there were Chile and, later, Nicaragua.

This tendency of seeing all reformist movements in the Third World as potential East-West conflicts has had its ebb and flow over the years. The

Cuban revolution and the missile crisis several years later certainly colored the image of U.S.-Soviet relations and the U.S. policy position in Latin America throughout the 1960s. The Vietnam war was further evidence that the Soviet Union could indeed cause trouble and embarrassment for the United States in the Third World. In the 1970s there developed an accommodating stance on both sides—*détente*, as it was called. But this was not to last. After the Iranian revolution and the Soviet invasion of Afghanistan, relations between the United States and the USSR steadily deteriorated, and U.S. reactions to issues in the Third World (especially Central America) again assumed an East-West, cold war outlook. In the past several years, a new détente has emerged following some initiatives of both the Soviet Union and the United States.

Gothlieb (1987) recently reviewed some highlights in the cold war chronologically: the McCarthy era, Vietnam, the Reagan military buildup. He concludes that

> there is a substantial body of U.S. opinion that believes the nation is always too lax, or on the edge of being too lax, about communism. . . . Somehow, it does not seem to matter how vigilant the nation is about communism; some people will always think it is lax. . . . But it would be nice if, after 40 years of this Cold War business, we could finally get the hang of it and settle into a vigilance of a level that is self-serving, not self-defeating.

Thiesenhusen (1989b), commenting on a piece by Robert White (1985), former U.S. ambassador to El Salvador, concludes that:

> White appears to be asserting that the United States does not want the Nicaraguan revolution to be successful under any conditions, for that will make Central America less dependent on the United States and, hence, less controllable. White not only criticizes the Republican regime, but extends his remarks to critique all post–World War II U.S. administrations. (494)

On issues of internal structural reforms, particularly in Latin America, the United States finds itself in an especially difficult position. As William Fulbright reminded his fellow Senators in 1965, "if we are automatically to oppose any reform movement that communists adhere to, we are likely to end up opposing every reform movement, making ourselves the prisoners of reactionaries who wish to preserve the status quo—and the status quo in many countries is not good enough" (Congressional Record 1965, 23855).

The reforms in Japan, Taiwan, and South Korea by and large did not have to contend with U.S. corporate interests, as would those fifteen or twenty years later in Latin America. As Penn (1961) explains,

We tend to think of United States firms as going into foreign countries and operating pretty much as they do in the United States, with labor and capital sharing the same rights and responsibilities as they do in the United States. Generally, however, this is not the case. When a company acquires property in another country it will generally follow the rules of that country. . . . It may furnish better than average facilities and conditions of employment for its laborers. Yet a United States company in a feudal country becomes a symbol of the general ownership structure of the past and, as such, the target of land reform programs. To put it bluntly, United States industry cannot operate in a feudal country without accepting the rules of feudalism and thus sharing the villain's role for those who want to strengthen the economic and legal position of the landless and jobless. (101)

Land Reform, Private Property, and Free Markets

Some argue against land reform in terms of the near-sacred rights of private property. It has been said that private property is a right ordained by natural law, and that any attack on it is an attack on society and its most basic unit, the family. Private property, it is sometimes claimed, is the pillar of a civilized society. If these premises are accepted, then it must likewise be admitted that property cannot perform these laudable functions if most people are without it. Private property is, of course, a creation of the state. Feudal lords, in the absence of the nation-state, had to have their own armies to protect "their property."

Nations place many restrictions on private property. In the United States, the local, state, or national government can change the rules governing a landowner's use of his property. The government can also, with appropriate compensation, take title to privately owned land for public purposes. Finally, the government's power to tax and to spend certainly impinges on the ownership and use of property in many ways. The key to protecting individual rights to property lies in political institutions which require that rules be reasonable and not arbitrary, necessary for the purpose imposed, and carried out by due process of law. Where such political institutions are absent, current landowners may have acquired their ownership by arbitrary measures and may indeed have used the powers of government for their own personal purposes. In fact, in some countries of Latin America there are ongoing efforts for the "search and recovery" of national lands for which current "owners" or claimants may not have valid titles. Some of these lands, it is claimed, were given illegally by previous regimes and are really state—not private—lands (AID 1989).

There has been and there remains, throughout Latin America, a strong public interest in the expanded rights of access to and use of land, water, and other natural resources. This should not be interpreted as opposition to private property—far from it! What is at issue here is the concentration of property under private control versus its wider distribution. What is also at issue is an inability, in some countries, to enforce the legitimate public interest in private property. Private property is not and cannot be an absolute right. Questions of property always involve a dual relation of private and public purposes (Commons 1957, 326–27): Always, the question is not just "*What* is a private purpose over and against a public purpose?" But more than that, "Is the private purpose *also* a public purpose, or *merely* a private purpose?"

It is not very helpful, nor is it accurate, to say that private property and enterprise made the United States great and that this is what the United States has to offer in the struggle for economic development around the world. In fact, it is our open and flexible political system that has allowed us to make private enterprise *within the United States* consistent with the general public interest, as Marx thought it never could be. However, there is no reason to expect that private enterprise will automatically function in the public interest in a system lacking these political institutions and the middle-class society on which they rest.

We need to be aware that market forces and private enterprise function well in the United States because of (1) a very broad distribution of resources and assets, and (2) the ability of people to organize and influence policy and thus, through these actions, to gain access to recources and income-earning opportunities.

Even here, of course, we know that private enterprise and free market forces leave many people on the outside looking in. But it is this relatively wide distribution and access *plus* our open and flexible political institutions that have permitted private enterprise in the United States to be reasonably consistent with the general public interest. An important question in every case is whether land, capital, and product markets are or can be made sufficiently free and open in agrarian countries to achieve development through incentive-oriented policy without direct public interventions such as land reform.

Free markets are wonderful in an economy with the characteristics that allow them to operate effectively. But market forces are a function of economic power and control. When economic resources and opportunities are widely distributed, then most economic activity can best be left to individual, private initiative and to market forces. This is not necessarily true where a skewed distribution of resources and opportunities makes self-help impossible for a large, desperately poor proportion of a society. Under these conditions, market forces will marginalize an increasing proportion of the people with no correcting forces except government intervention. In fact, where land reform becomes an issue, the situation may indeed reflect the consequences of market forces operating in a system with a highly skewed distribution of resources and opportunities.

The Alliance for Progress and Land Reform

Although agrarian reform in Latin America is an old issue, with early roots in the Mexican revolution and the Mexican Constitution of 1917, it became a general political issue throughout the region in the 1960s. The Cuban revolution under Fidel Castro had introduced a radical land reform in that Caribbean island. Several years later, President John F. Kennedy's administration pushed for reforms via the Alliance for Progress. For reasons Galbraith (1951) cites and because of the U.S. policy dilemma discussed earlier, the expectations of the Alliance were unrealistic. The Alliance produced the following declaration (Inter-American Economic and Social Council 1961) committing the signatories to enhanced development, including changes in land tenure:

> To encourage, in accordance with the characteristics of each country, programs of comprehensive agrarian reform leading to effective transformation, where required, of unjust structures and systems of land tenure and use, with a view to replacing latifundia and dwarf holdings by an equitable system of land tenure so that, with the help of timely and adequate credit, technical assistance, and facilities for the marketing and distribution of products, the land will become for the man who works it the basis of his economic stability, the foundation of his increasing welfare, and the guarantee of his freedom and dignity. (3)

Most Latin American countries subsequently passed agrarian reform laws, but the promised changes were not realized fully anywhere. Neither the declaration nor the laws it spawned took adequate account of the deep political opposition to fundamental change which prevailed throughout the region. Legislation does not guarantee substantive action and follow-through. The United States has very little leverage to induce other sovereign governments to act aggressively on these complex, politically sensitive matters. An outside power, no matter how dominant economically or militarily, cannot control another country's policies on such issues as land reform.

The Alliance envisioned (or assumed) ideal conditions: a government with strong leadership firmly committed to reform, effective rural/peasant organizations supporting the reform and able to play a key role in its implementation, an efficient and responsive agricultural bureaucracy, accurate and readily available records of land ownership, accurate land-use and land-classification maps, a well-developed infrastructure including functional markets and adequate systems of transport and communication, and so forth. But, of course, these conditions did not exist anywhere in Latin America.

It should be noted that land tenure institutions have unique features growing out of historical patterns of settlement or conquest. Such institutions are tied to value systems and grounded in religious, social, political, and cultural antecedents. Changes that work well in one setting may be totally unworkable in another. Likewise, an institution is not defined by its name but rather by the function, procedures, rights, duties, restraints, and privileges that it embodies within the complex web of institutions that makes up a sociocultural-political system. A farm corporation in Iran is in no way comparable to a farm corporation in southern California. A tenant farmer growing corn in central Illinois has much more in common with an owner-operator on the neighboring farm than with a tenant farmer growing corn in central Luzon. Tenancy, sharecropping, owner-operatorship, partnerships, corporations, and production cooperatives in various parts of the world are not comparable institutions simply because they are called by the same name. More serious is the mistaken assumption that institutions function everywhere as they do in the United States—or, worse still, as they are romanticized in our folklore. Researchers, as well as policy-oriented agencies, have to struggle to retain clear perspectives. It requires, says Patch (1965),

> a willingness to immerse oneself in a strange culture, maintaining sympathy without losing objectivity, forming opinions about the feasibility of alternative courses without becoming passionate, understanding political and practical considerations without becoming involved in them, and emerging with ideas of what is possible and what is impossible within the whole web of . . . culture and behavior. (5)

A Comment on the Chapters That Follow

Chapter 2 of this monograph summarizes some key ideological, theoretical, and socioeconomic ideas and perspectives, the arguments and counterarguments about land reform, that prevailed going into the 1960s as well as those that emerged in the following several decades. Chapter 3 gives a brief summary of the land reforms implemented in Latin America over the past three decades, along with an evaluation of achievements. Chapter 4 reviews demographic and economic trends in Latin America over the past several decades. In light of the progress and changes revealed, the question is raised whether reform is, in fact, still needed. Chapter 5 discusses measures related to land reform: land registration and titling, land taxation, and land transfer and financing mechanisms. Finally, chapter 6 looks at forms of support which outside agencies might supply either to land reform per se or to a variety of other measures directed at restructuring land markets and rural institutions.

2

Theoretical and Ideological Perspectives

An important phenomenon after World War II was decolonization and the achievement of political independence by Third World countries. In the social sciences, this led to a rediscovery and reinterpretation of the term *development*. As the meaning of development was broadened to encompass more than economic growth, contemporary explanations of development came under scrutiny. The ideological and analytical concepts they embodied were often said to give an inadequate and misleading view of the historical evolution of social, economic, and political structures in the nonindustrialized societies.

Land reform was not an integral part of all these theories and explanations. Nor was decolonization directly relevant in most of Latin America in the 1950s and 1960s. However, the debate over theories of development has been an active one in Latin America, and it has greatly affected the way reform issues are formulated and the means by which reform objectives are pursued. Competing views of development include several formulations—structuralism, dependency, institutionalism, and liberation theology, among others—that reflect a loss of confidence in prevailing concepts of development, especially the economic growth-modernization paradigm.

Structuralism

Doubts about the neoclassical economic view of international free trade and development signaled the rise of structuralism in development thought. In the 1950s, some observers began to question the merits of free trade as the engine of growth for underdeveloped countries. Under the existing division of labor in the global economic system, they argued, countries of the periphery produced and exported raw materials to countries of the center, which in turn specialized in manufactured goods. The periphery, as a result, was always subject to deteriorating terms of trade and a chronic slowdown in domestic capital accumulation. The gains from international free trade based on comparative advantage were concentrated in the center; continued reliance on the export of primary products could not serve as a major stimulus for development (Singer 1950; Prebisch 1950).

This notion (also known as the *Prebisch-Singer thesis*) claimed that in the longer run, "backwash effects" from free trade might even lead to worsening economic and social conditions in the periphery (Myrdal 1957). An expanded export market would favor the countries with developed industries, while countries with a small industrial base would fall behind in competition with their developed counterparts. Free trade, in Myrdal's view, ran the risk of aggravating rather than reducing income differences among countries. International free trade might generate certain "spread effects" in the short run, but these were likely to be eroded by "backwash effects" in the long run.

Structuralism concentrated on the structure of markets, technological progress, and the characteristics of primary and manufactured goods vis-à-vis production and demand. The competitive international market for primary products meant that technological progress would have quite opposite impacts on prices, wages, and profits in the center versus the periphery. The structuralists argued that technological progress in the center is accompanied by reduced production costs, higher profits, and higher wages as a result of the countervailing power of industrial oligopolies and strong labor unions. However, increased efficiency and reduced production costs in the periphery would result only in lower export prices. On the demand side, the different income elasticities for primary and manufactured goods automatically work in favor of the center (Prebisch 1950).

This version of the structuralist thesis looked to import substitution as a remedy to this terms-of-trade dilemma, without specific focus on land tenure and reform. There was, however, another structuralist approach. In this formulation, the low productivity of agriculture and its unresponsiveness to economic incentives due to the *latifundio/minifundio* system of ownership and organization led to rising food prices and inflation. In this view, "the patterns of land tenure and ownership are held responsible for the lag in agricultural output" (Hirschman 1963, 215); consequently, land-tenure reform is recommended.[1]

---

1.   Hirschman outlines other major tenets of this structuralist approach and cites papers by Roberto Campos, David Felix, and Joseph Grünwald, which appear in his earlier book (Hirschman 1961). The book by Meier (1964) is also a good source for various theoretical positions on economic development.

Dependency

Policies based on structuralism, often associated with the Economic Commission for Latin America (ECLA), emphasized, as noted above, import-substituting industrialization. In the 1960s, many shortcomings of these policies became obvious. Economic growth was stagnating, even in the more industrialized nations of Latin America. Domestic markets showed little expansion; growth in purchasing power was limited to certain social strata. On the other hand, conventional exports had been neglected. Import dependency on capital goods took the place of import dependency on consumer goods. The result was a serious balance-of payments problem. ECLA was no longer able to hold onto its optimism about Latin American development: "In Latin America . . . there is a general consciousness of living through a period of decline. . . . The phase of 'easy' development, through increasing exports of primary products or through import substitution, has everywhere been exhausted" (Hirschman 1968, citing Furtado 1966). This sense of pessimism was enough to radicalize even some ECLA veterans (notably Furtado and Sunkel), who joined in formulating the dependency school of thought.

Dependency theorists come from different disciplines and perspectives, so here also two rather distinct views emerged. They are expressed mainly in terms of prospects for political action. One stems from ECLA's structuralist perspective and is seen as a deepening of that viewpoint. The other originated with the Marxist scholars who broke with the stultifying dogmatism of the Stalinist heritage (O'Brien 1975). Sunkel (1969, 1971), Sunkel and Paz (1973), Sunkel and Fuenzalida (1979), and Furtado (1963, 1965, 1970) are among the chief architects of the former, while Marini (1965, 1972), Dos Santos (1970, 1973), and Frank (1967, 1969) are identified with the latter. There are others (for example, Cardoso [1972], and Stavenhagen [1981]) who seem to work from both neostructuralist and Marxist foundations.

In criticizing the modernization paradigm, dependency theorists agree in challenging its definition of development, its universal applicability, and its analytical approach. They say that the symptoms of underdevelopment—low income; slow growth; unemployment; income inequality; regional imbalances; and cultural, social, economic, and political marginalization—are not just simple deviations from an ideal pattern of growth and modernization. Rather, these problems are the consequences of a formal system with two mutually reinforcing, interdependent structures that underlie the historical development of global capitalism. This global perspective and the historical process of capitalist development form key elements in the basic hypothesis of dependency theory, which views development and underdevelopment as partial, interdependent structures in a single system.

A dependent relationship exists when some countries can develop through self-impulsion, whereas others, being in a dependent position, can grow only in response to the expansion of the dominant countries (Dos Santos 1973). This process is replicated internally in the dependent countries. Thus at the international level, the advanced economic centers will extract surplus value from the peripheral countries while, within the dependent countries, the metropolitan centers will extract surplus from the hinterland. This internal aspect of dependency is often referred to as *internal colonialism* (Dos Santos 1970, 234; Sunkel 1971; O'Brien 1975, 14).

Underdevelopment cannot be understood as a phase to be followed by a development process that replicates the experience of the dominant center countries. According to dependency theory, development and underdevelopment can be understood only as two aspects of the same historical process involving the creation and spread of modern technology (Furtado 1970, xvi). It is incorporation into the global capitalist system that leads to the "development of underdevelopment" in the periphery. "Capitalism's essential internal contradiction between exploiting and exploited," says Frank (1969, 226), acts to produce simultaneous development and underdevelopment.

Stavenhagen (1981) also argues that the economic backwardness of Latin America (and other Third World nations) can best be understood as internal colonialism—the internal colonies (backward regions or groups) performing the same functions within a country as do the Latin American nations as "colonies" of the United States and other industrialized countries.

Dependency theory with its extension to internal colonialism does find a major role for land reform. Stavenhagen (1981) argues that the structure of internal colonialism "must be broken in order to get out of the vicious cycle of poverty, backwardness, external dependence, and internal domination. The great problem posed by Latin America today is how to break this vicious cycle" (39). In terms of economic performance, the most prominent victims of internal colonialism are the poor and the landless or near-landless in the agricultural sector. The internal land tenure system must be changed because it determines many of the interrelationships among choice of technology, production of a salable surplus, and income distribution. In the periphery, says Prebisch (1980), "industrialization is superimposed on a land tenure regime which acts as a brake on the penetration of techniques and productivity, to the detriment of development" (183). But the power of internal domination comes not only from control over land. Traditional landowners have joined with modern commercial and industrial entrepreneurs to form the present ruling classes. Although dependency theory does call for redistributive land reforms, it recognizes that political prospects for reform became more remote when the traditional landowning class joined forces with the modern industrial class.

Institutionalism

The institutional economists who proposed the "economic case for land reform" in the early 1970s (see Dorner, ed. 1971) also saw shortcomings in traditional development theory, especially the misleading identification of increases in real per capita output with development. The focus on gross output diverted attention from equally important issues of social equity: poverty, unemployment, and political powerlessness. The motive for reassessing traditional theory was easy to ascertain: impressive increases in growth for certain agricultural commodities in Latin America in the 1960s had been accompanied by a disturbing rise in rural and urban unemployment and poverty (Carter and Jonakin 1987).

The institutionalists' reformulation of development theory indicated that both growth and equity could and should occur together. Dorner and Kanel (1971) not only challenged the growth theorists' assertions about how best to promote production, but also held out the promise for a simultaneous advance in social equity.

This theory is built around three elements—two empirically based propositions about supply and demand and one assumption about the need for state intervention. The supply-side component of the theory is grounded in the observation that an inverse relation exists between farm size and productivity. If output per unit of land is indeed greater on holdings of smaller size, then policy implications are immediate and dramatic. Land reforms that distribute public lands or redistribute land from large estates, thereby creating many new family farms, would not only boost aggregate production but would also establish greater equity. Because large-scale agriculture frequently displaces labor at a rate faster than industry can employ it, the creation of relatively small family farms (or cooperative forms of tenure) would provide employment for excess labor, relieve the pressures of urban migration, and release labor in a more controlled and beneficial way.

The theory also maintains that a change in the composition of demand would occur among the low-income rural majority as their incomes rose, a direct benefit from land reform. This change involves a high income elasticity of demand for industrial goods and, consequently, vital linkages between the growing manufacturing sector and the reenergized farm sector. These supply- and demand-side factors would together result in an integrated process of agricultural-industrial development. According to this view,

> This [institutionalist] policy approach produces the required increases in agricultural production and avoids displacing labor prematurely from agriculture. It is a prescription for agricultural research, for large increases in the use of yield-increasing inputs such as fertilizer, improved seeds, insecticides and pesticides, for increases in irrigation facilities, and for building service institutions in extension, marketing, and credit. It is also a prescription to minimize mechanization, especially when it serves to displace labor. (Dorner and Kanel 1971, 45)

Of course, this policy (see also Johnston and Mellor 1961) depends on a land reform that enfranchises smallholders and/or establishes cooperative tenure forms (Dorner 1972). The explicit recognition of a particular regime of policies to promote growth with equity introduced the third element of the institutionalist argument—the necessity of state intervention in a systematic and enduring way.

Liberation Theology

Yet another line of thought arising in Latin America during the 1960s and later was labeled *liberation theology* because it originated primarily with Catholic theologians. Several meetings of Latin American Catholic bishops provided a fundamental rationale from the standpoint of the Church for this approach to the issues of poverty and for their potential cure. One of its basic tenets is that development alone is not sufficient unless it is humane and respects the interests of the disinherited masses (see, for example, Camara 1969; Moosbrugger and Weigner 1972; Vekemans 1964; and Dussel 1976). In essence, liberation theology provides a new critical interpretation of history and asks Christians to involve themselves in constructing values in consort with groups that represent the wishes of the people (Goulet 1974).

To achieve a humane pattern of development, say the liberation theologians, superficial reform is absolutely insufficient: "What is needed is a reform in depth, a profound and rapid change; what we must achieve—let's not be afraid of the word—is a structural revolution" (Camara 1969, 102). In some sense and in some areas, however, a structural revolution has been in progress in Latin America, led not by the Church but by the Marxists. Many reformists, including dissident members of the Church, have joined these revolutionaries. The situation led Vekemans (1964) to argue that efforts at superficial reform may bring short-term benefits and postpone an explosion, but if the need for basic change is not realized, this explosion will nevertheless occur. And the longer the change is delayed, the more violent the explosion will be. Without a thorough and quick social change on a truly revolutionary scale, says Vekemans, there is no chance of responding adequately to the revolutionary crisis that threatens the region.

Liberation theology rejects capitalism as immoral and as structurally incompatible with social justice; even liberal capitalism has its own materialistic roots and is directly responsible for the international dictatorship of economic power (Camara 1969, 1979; Dussel 1976). Liberation theologians advocate socialism. Their version of socialism is free from materialism and quite unrelated to Marxism. Máspero (1964), for instance, argues that "the social revolution in Latin America must be a moral revolution. It must embody a set of values and a concept of man and society that will result in human liberation and lead toward continuity and stability. We must reject all movements that might militate against the dignity of man" (176). Camara (1969) said that "the best way to combat Marxism is to teach a religion which is not 'the opium of the people'; to preach a Christianity which, in union with Christ and following his example, embodies and appropriates all human problems in order to accomplish man's redemption" (75). In the 1971 Synod, the Peruvian bishops declared, "Christians ought to opt for socialism. We do not mean a bureaucratic, totalitarian, or atheistic socialism; we mean a socialism that is both humanistic and Christian" (quoted in Dussel 1976, 134).

The new theologians defend private property but reject the idea that the right to private property is *natural* and *inalienable*. "Only what is necessary for man's end is a natural right; all else is not," says Dussel (1976, 137), and everything beyond necessity (second car, second home, and so on), if attained by depriving others, is unmistakably against the doctrine of Christian tradition. "How far can we go in defending private property?" asks Camara (1969). "To the point of leaving the masses of people without the barest necessities? No, this is not justice in my opinion" (45).

The liberation theologians identify an educative role for the Church. The 1971 Synod of Peruvian Bishops declared that "the mission of the Church is to open people's minds and hearts to consideration of the most pressing and urgent problems" (quoted in Dussel 1976, 135).

The new theologians know that "whoever rises up and demands human and social advancement . . . [can] expect with certainty to be considered and opposed as a subversive and a communist" (Camara 1969, 34). Dussel (1976) goes farther: "We cannot continue to live tranquilly within the established order, for that established order is grounded on sin and unjust domination. . . . If the established order is grounded on domination of other human beings, then it should not be respected. To obey laws that are part of such an order is to commit sin. There are times when the legal order turns into an established immorality, when few legal actions are morally good. Within the context of an unjust totality, illegal actions may be good" (144).

Liberation theology makes land reform a major issue. The new theologians argue that reforms to date have failed to solve the problems of the great mass of landless workers, tenants, and small-plot owners. Land monopoly and feudalism in labor relations have persisted, especially in plantation agriculture (sugarcane, coffee, bananas, and the like). Camara (1969) urges an authentic, large-scale land reform program for Latin America—not pilot projects or ineffectual colonization efforts. He recommends that CELAM (the Latin American Episcopal Conference) pay special attention to organizing peasants and small-plot owners for truly redistributive land reforms.

Postreform Interpretations

In looking back on the 1960s and 1970s from the vantage point of the 1980s, we see that new formulations have emerged. There have been rather profound changes in the economies of most Latin American countries over the past thirty years (as described in chapter 4). The agrarian structure, too, has changed—with and without reform. Population growth, market forces, various measures taken by governments—all have influenced these changes. The very threat of land expropriation and reform gave rise to a new economic responsiveness on the part of the large landowners, the *latifundistas*. As Carter and Mesbah (1990) suggest, "Both Lehmann (1978) and de Janvry (1981) describe important episodes of land reform in Latin America in these terms. The very success of those reforms, both in terms of redistribution and in terms of shaking large-scale agriculture out of its feudal torpor, spells, however, the end of land reform under this scenario"(12).

De Janvry is the chief advocate of one of the major postreform interpretations. His is a skeptical—indeed, cynical—view of the land reforms carried out in the 1960s and 1970s. Land reform is a device *not* to help the poor but to benefit the nonreformed sector—that is, the lands not touched directly by the reform. And it is true, of course, that this nonreformed sector retains by far the largest amount of agricultural land in almost all Latin American countries. Thus, by and large, the land reforms have had the effect, by design or otherwise, of encouraging the development of capitalist agriculture in the nonreformed sector, which often retains the best and most productive agricultural lands in the country. This sector also receives the bulk of the public services, such as credit, research and extension, production inputs, and infrastructure (de Janvry 1981, 214–18).

Since, with few exceptions, the political ideology in Latin American countries favors capitalism, there are a number of transitional "roads" from the precapitalist or feudal mode to the capitalist mode. The major paths of this transition, according to de Janvry, include the following. First, there is a transition from a Precapitalist Mode to Junker Road. *Junker* is the term applied by Lenin to the feudal lords of Prussia who transformed themselves into large capitalist farmers. In another transition, from a Precapitalist Mode to Farmer Road, the "Precapitalist estates are replaced by commercial farms as size limits are imposed on land ownership, and a reform sector is created" (de Janvry 1981, 209). There is also a Junker-Road-to-Farmer-Road transition, and a number of counterreform categories leading back to the precapitalist mode. Various Latin American reforms fall within each of these transition categories, although according to de Janvry, most of them fall within the first two listed.

De Janvry presents not so much a theory as an attempt to explain the complex changes, revolutions, and counterrevolutions that have occurred in Latin America. His position has been subjected to a number of criticisms. Barraclough (1984, 648–49) questions de Janvry's methodology and suggests that his elaborate theoretical framework seems only marginally relevant to his conclusions; Sen (1983, A–119) suggests that while the broad picture is not in question, there is often a lack of quantitative specification; and Schuh (1984) questions the labor theory of value underlying de Janvry's analysis. Nevertheless, a number of de Janvry's explanations and interpretations do at times correspond rather well with what has occurred in Latin America.

Some doubts have also been expressed with respect to the continuing economic importance of the land resource. If land is actually declining in significance vis-à-vis capital and technology, perhaps redistributive land reforms are outmoded in the world of today. Bromley (1984) notes that "a plethora of changes have occurred in the developing economies which, in combination, drive down the economic role of land to the point that in some instances access to—or control over—land may be quite irrelevant. . . . The advent of high-yielding varieties, increased reliance on chemical pesticides and fertilizers, control over irrigation water . . . all combine to render—in many instances—land ownership quite irrelevant" (275–76).

We should distinguish between an agrarian system and an industrial system when addressing the question of the declining importance of agricultural landownership. Land as a factor of production does indeed decline in importance as capital embodied in various technological substances, processes, and devices assumes a much larger role, and Bromley does modify the statement by qualifications such as "in some" or "in many" instances. These are certainly key modifiers of the conclusion about the irrelevancy of landownership. We should also note that *ownership* per se may be much less relevant in an open and a relatively free market system where purchase-sale and rental markets for land are active and accessible. When these conditions do not hold, however, in societies where land reform becomes an issue, one would be hard pressed to find a single landowner or one who is seeking land who would admit that landownership is irrelevant. Case studies sponsored by the World Bank in Thailand show major increases in both land values and land-use intensity following the issuance of clear and legally state-sanctioned land titles (Feder et al. 1986), and an earlier study on Costa Rica (Salas et al. 1970) reached the same conclusions.

The Nature and Status of the Inverse Relation between Farm Size and Productivity

The economic rationale underlying several of the above positions on land reform (and most explicitly the institutionalist approach) rests on the observation that small farms generally have a higher value of output per unit of land and capital than do large farms (that is, operating units, measured in land area). This was clearly portrayed with data from the 1960s for a number of Asian and Latin American countries (Dorner 1972, 119–24). Even the postreform, unimodal, small-farm systems of Japan and Taiwan continued to show this inverse relation to some degree; it was also found in some cases where the smallest categories of farmers represented tenants and sharecroppers. Some discussion and speculation suggests that the green revolution may have changed this relationship. If it has been greatly altered, so that large farms now outproduce smaller ones on a per-acre or per-hectare basis, part of the rationale for breaking up large units would no longer be valid.

Some new thinking has also been expressed on sharecropping, allowing that there might be positive features to this tenure form. To the classical and neoclassical economists, sharecropping provides the farmer with less incentive to work and is therefore a less efficient arrangement than that of either a fixed-rent tenant or an owner-cultivator. This position was reexamined in the early 1950s, and the major conclusion to emerge was that "there is no substitute, from the standpoint of sheer productivity, and irrespective of sociological considerations, for an owner-operated agricultural system" (Hayami and Ruttan 1985, 389–90, quoting Drake 1952, 549). In this section we consider some of the new ideas and literature on these questions.

With respect to the basic proposition of the inverse relation between farm size and productivity, it has been suggested, for example, that the size/productivity relation might be a result of rapid population growth in areas of high soil fertility and the consequent subdivision of land into smaller and smaller units of high productivity (Carter 1984, 136–37). Studies testing this hypothesis in India have concluded that soil fertility is indeed better on small farms, but that the inverse relation survives independently of this factor (Sen 1981, 204; Carter 1984, 139). Another hypothesis holds that the inverse relation between farm size and productivity could be a result of demographic changes in the size and composition of the peasant family. While this idea, too, has some explanatory value, the inverse relation again survives, even when family differences are factored out.

The principal variable that does, in fact, explain the inverse relation between farm size and productivity is failure (or imperfection) in factor markets. If imperfection existed only in the labor market, the small family farm with excess labor could achieve optimum allocation of its labor by resorting to perfect (or at least relatively well-functioning) markets in credit and land. It could lease the amount of land needed to keep farm size optimally proportional to family size. Labor inputs would be identical across farms because there would be no need for labor intensification, and yields per unit of land would be unaffected (Feder 1985, 311). In reality, however, land and labor misallocation arising in imperfect markets is the key to an inverse relation between farm size and productivity. Thus, the general recommendations for land redistribution are consistent with the market failure hypothesis. Land reform attempts to repair these market failures and to make land, labor, and credit markets more competitive. According to Carter and Jonakin (1987),

> The inverse relation arises from (1) involuntary unemployment, which lowers the [real cost of the peasant family's own labor]. The involuntary unemployment itself results from credit markets which limit the peasant family's ability to rent in land. Labor intensificaiton on the family plot results. . . . (2) supervisory, or control, problems which limit the use of hired labor on larger farms, thereby contributing to labor intensification on the family-labor farm. (10–11)

Jonakin and Carter also looked at the literature of the past twenty years in an attempt to determine whether an inverse relation between farm size and output per unit of land has persisted in the presence of green revolution inputs and mechanization. According to one set of studies, based almost exclusively in India, post–green revolution data present ambiguous conclusions (Deolalikar 1981; Saini 1971; Rao 1975; Bardhan 1973). In some cases, the inverse relation was maintained; in others, it was weakened or even reversed. Green revolution inputs used in combination with mechanization seem to weaken the inverse relation. On the other hand, the relation between farm size and intensity of labor use continues to be negative (Sen 1981; Ghose 1979).

Sen (1981) argues that these trends are explicable as structural adaptations to multiple-market failures and to technological innovation in agriculture:

> Because small farmers could not always use as much fertilizer etc. as bigger farmers, their output has grown proportionately less and the size-productivity relation has been *weakened*. The fact that the inverse relationship between farm size and labour use has, simultaneously, been *strengthened* suggests that problems such as supervision have come in the way of intensification on many of the larger farms. In some cases mechanisation has allowed a way round supervision problems, but, in others (sharecropping), output increases must have been held back. (344–45)

Deolalikar (1981, 278) suggests that these circumstances require policies giving small farmers greater access to credit and thus to increased use of the new inputs. These, of course, are much the same recommendations ordinarily made by advocates of land reform and the creation of additional small farms operated with family labor.

If the green revolution has indeed weakened or reversed the inverse relation between farm size and productivity, it could be concluded that a land reform creating small, labor-intensive farms would have an adverse effect on efficiency, even while equity might be served. But one must be very cautious here. An emphasis on *private efficiency* for the larger farms must be weighed against the *social inefficiency* of unemployed and underemployed labor. This labor may have a social opportunity cost of zero or even less. As long as the small farm uses more labor and produces at least as much output per unit of land, it is likely to be more efficient from the standpoint of social accounts than the larger unit using less labor and more capital (the latter having a very high opportunity cost). Even a lower output per unit of land on the small farm does not automatically suggest lower social efficiency.

Looking at Mexico's farm economy of the 1960s, Dovring (1969) concludes that

> since the land and the farm labor are free goods, from the viewpoint of the national economy, it appears that small-scale, labor-intensive production is less costly than large-scale production in terms of goods that are scarce in the Mexican economy. The large private farms are using more of the hardware that might otherwise have been invested toward even more rapid industrialization of the country. . . . The surprising fact is that ejido production is cheaper, in social-account opportunity cost, than large-scale private-farm production. . . . There is no doubt that the owners or holders of large private farms make a good income by using more machines and somewhat less labor, but they render a less useful service to the struggling developing economy of a low-income, capital-scarce country. (21–22)

Studies reporting the disappearance or weakening of the inverse relation are from Asia, mainly from India. Recent studies in Latin America, as well as others in India, do continue to show a strong inverse relation between farm size and output per unit of land.

The general conclusion of Berry and Cline's (1979) research in Latin America (Brazil and Colombia) and Asia (India, Pakistan, the Philippines, and Malaysia) showed that in the presence of green revolution technologies, the smaller the farm size, the greater the land productivity and the total social factor productivity. (Social factor productivity relates total output to the value of factor inputs as evaluated at *social* prices, where social price for land is calculated at a certain per annum percentage opportunity cost and where the social price for labor is established by a regional minimum wage [Berry and Cline 1979, 54].)

Using farm-survey data for Brazil (1962–63 and 1973 for northeast Brazil), they concluded that "output per farm area declines as farm size rises, even after taking account of land quality; that labor is replaced by land and capital as farm size rises" (Berry and Cline 1979, 58).[2] They also observed that the degree of change over time in the inverse relation between farm size and land productivity varied considerably from one country to another and between the continents.

In Brazil there was little change, if any, during the 1960s, and in Colombia the degree of land utilization for large farms was still far below that of small farms by the end of the decade. Large farms in Pakistan and India, however, did experience improvement in relative land productivity, but it still remained below that of small farms, especially in India, by the early 1970s. According to Berry and Cline (1979), "The somewhat greater improvement in Pakistan and India than in Brazil and Colombia presumably reflects the much greater impact of the Green Revolution in Asia than in Latin America" (127).

In a recent study, Thiesenhusen and Melmed-Sanjak (1990), using census data, were able to look at a number of changing relationships in Brazilian agriculture. Table 1 is reproduced from this study. It continues to show, on an aggregate bases for all of Brazil, a very marked inverse relation for productivity of land (agricultural and cropland) as well as for capital. Total receipts per labor unit, as always, show the opposite relation.

In India, Bhalla (1979) found that not only was there a negative relation

2. Barry and Cline (1979, 67) do dismiss the striking confirmation of the inverse relation in Colombia because large farms there were mostly nonmodern "holdouts" in "zones of colonization," whereas small farms were unrepresentatively chosen from among the most favored in terms of land quality and access to government credit programs.

Table 1.   Relationship between Land, Labor, and Capital Productivities, Brazil, 1980
(expressed as percentages of the "Under 1 hectare" category)

Farm Size (in hectares)	Total Receipts per			
	Agricultural Land Hectare	Cropland Hectare	Labor Unit	Capital Unit
Under 1	100	100	100	100
1–10	35	70	184	88
10–50	18	67	428	72
50–200	9	59	658	59
200–2,000	6	57	1,290	51
2,000–10,000	3	48	2,230	27
10,000 and over	1	35	1,950	22
National	7	61	—	55

Source: *Censo Agropecuário, 1980*, Tables 18, 20, 22, 29, 32, and 34. From Thiesenhusen and Melmed-Sanjak (1990, 403).

between size and productivity at the aggregate level, but also "that this relationship remains significant even after differences in land quality, irrigation, and cropping patterns are allowed for" (154).

The persistence of the inverse relation in these cases echoes earlier arguments about multiple-market failures. Explanations for the differential factor intensities across farm sizes in Brazil and India point to discrepancies in factor prices confronting farms of varying size. As before, the precise loci of these market failures are the different prices attached to land, credit, and labor, and the underlying cause is, of course, the relative concentration of resources and economic power, making some people "much more equal" than others.

With respect to land, Berry and Cline (1979) argue that economies of scale operate in the purchasing of land. The effect of these economies on the inverse relation would be difficult to predict. Inasmuch as land is cheaper for large farms the value of output net of cost is enhanced, and the inverse relation weakened. On the other hand, the higher cost of land for the small farmer discourages land purchases and concentrates labor on existing small plots. Inasmuch as the intensity of labor use on small farms is increased relative to large farms, the inverse relation is strengthened.

More important, cheaper credit for larger farms reinforces their tendency to reduce labor use. Different real interest rates reflect the privileged access that large farmers have to "special government credit programs or machinery import subsidy programs" (Berry and Cline 1979, 10). Small farmers must instead resort more often to high-interest loans provided by traditional moneylenders.[3] The impact of these differential prices is, again, to promote a relatively greater use of labor on the small farms.

The most significant aspect of multiple-market failure, according to Bhalla (1979), is dualism in the labor market and the wage differential between small and large farms. But the fact of dualism—which implies that the marginal product of labor is higher on larger farms—begs the question of why the small farmer does not hire himself out to capture the gains from working for the large farmer. Bhalla explains that there is no 100 percent probability of employment, and Sen (1981) observes that peasants *are* deeply involved in labor markets but frequently confront "involuntary unemployment." This unemployment, along with personal contractual arrangements (sharecropping), imply the significance of supervisory costs in encouraging labor-market dualism. The result, again, is to promote more intensive labor use on the small farms.

Carter and Jonakin (1987) emphasize, after examining all the case studies, that whatever the "empirical findings with respect to the inverse relation . . . there is no real dispute that failures in land, credit, and labor markets are seen as having contributed most to its appearance" (26).

Discussion of an inverse relation between farm size and output must also deal with sharecropping as a tenure form. If large landowners would choose to parcel their land and operate with sharecroppers, would not the equity and productivity gains be similar to those obtained from a small owner-operated system of family farms?

New research and rethinking on the issue of sharecropping has shown that it is not always or necessarily an exploitative relationship.

> The literature on tenancy and agrarian contractual structure argues that share tenancy is not necessarily an inefficient feudal remnant but that it may represent the best contractual response to an imperfect market environment. In this *qualified sense* sharecropping can be an efficient institution. But it is important to recognize that this claim for the contingent efficiency of sharecropping is fundamentally distinct from . . . claims that share tenancy is efficient in an unqualified, global sense. First of all, sharecropping may cease to be an efficient or desirable way to organize production following changes in technology or market structure. The agrarian structure literature also admits the possibility that *comprehensive* tenancy reforms could in fact improve economic efficiency over that attained under sharecropping. However, just as important, that literature indicates that less comprehensive land

---

3.   Berry and Cline (1979) do not directly address credit rationing in laissez-faire credit markets. Here small farmers face higher capital costs as a result of their perceived riskiness, itself a function of the lower value of owned assets and "adverse selection" effects (Carter 1988). The question of high implicit rates of interest as a function of undervalued collateral is also neglected (Basu 1984).

reform can have ambiguous effects even on the welfare of its beneficiaries. Reforms undertaken without efforts to correct imperfections in market access and existence which underlie sharecropping may be counterproductive. . . . It should be emphasized that the fact that sharecropping and market interlinkages fulfill economic functions does not rule out the possibility that they are part of an exploitative relationship. (Carter and Kanel 1985, 8–9)[4]

If tenants or sharecroppers have the possibility of moving into other employment, agricultural or otherwise, landlords lose sole power over their opportunity structure; in that case sharecropping can be efficient and equitable. On the other hand, if a new technology with substantial payoff comes along, landlords may be able to reserve this for themselves and capture the full benefit simply by changing the tenure structure, eliminating the sharecropper, and operating the land with hired labor. In the United States in the 1930s, when the first Agricultural Adjustment Administration came into being, payments made to farm owners were supposed to be shared with tenants and sharecroppers. But the landlords, in order to reap more benefit, dismissed tenants and sharecroppers or transformed them into wage labor. This is the kind of possibility that must be considered. If sharecropping as a tenure form is to offer the same security and efficiency as owner-operated farms or long-term leases, external conditions must be favorable: there must be truly competitive markets and an opportunity structure that prevents undue influence by one party. With an open and competitive economy, with alternatives and opportunities for both sharecropper and landlord, sharecropping may be able to function as effectively as owner-operated farms.

Some Ideas from Macro Theory

Macroeconomic development theory has been used to suggest that a worsening income distribution in the early stages of economic growth may be normal. Kuznets (1955, 1966), while not necessarily drawing policy implications, has demonstrated that reduction in income inequality is a function of time. The inequality index follows an inverted U: income inequality tends to increase in the early stages of development, then levels off, and then decreases in later stages.

Experience shows however, that basic reforms can improve the income share of the poor as well as the growth of the economy. The widely heralded capitalist development and land reforms in Japan, South Korea, and Taiwan

4. Additional evidence on many of these issues is presented in Hayami and Kikuchi (1981); see also Lehmann (1986).

cannot be ignored as mere coincidences. In all cases, economic growth followed major agrarian reforms. In Taiwan, for instance, the income of the lower-percentile groups improved after a certain turning point in the inverted U-shaped curve proposed by Kuznets (Fei et al. 1978); this turning point was preceded by Taiwan's successful land reform. Reform provided a strong basis for improved earning among rural low-income people and offset any deterioration of their incomes in the process of growth.

The relationship between income inequality and growth varies not only between developed and less developed countries but also among less developed economies, depending upon their stage of development. Intercountry studies show that the less developed economies exhibit greater income inequality than the developed ones. Among the less developed countries, those with the lowest per capita incomes show *lower* inequality than the others. More generally, countries at an intermediate stage of development tend to show a more unequal income distribution than either richer or poorer countries (Kuznets 1966; Adelman and Morris 1973; Ahluwalia 1976).

According to Morawetz (1977), many of the countries that saw rapid, equitably distributed growth between 1950 and 1975 began the period with relatively equal asset distributions, while countries that had rapid but inequitably distributed growth began with sharply unequal distributions (World Bank 1975). In Morawetz's (1977) view,

> the *initial* distribution of assets and incomes may be an important determinant of the *trend* in inequality. Such a hypothesis makes some intuitive sense. People who own assets—whether physical or human capital—are best placed to profit once growth begins. Furthermore, both historical and simulative evidence suggest that the most powerful determinant of income distribution is the underlying structure of the enonomy; once growth is taking place, it seems to be difficult to effectively redistribute income through the use of "marginal" instruments such as taxation and public employment. These combined observations have potentially powerful implications: in particular, if equality is to be a short- to medium-term goal, it simply may not be possible to "grow first and redistribute later." Rather, it may be necessary to tackle asset redistribution as a first priority by whatever means are at hand. (71)

According to some macroeconomic analysts, the basic problem with many nations' development strategies is that governments have overvalued their currencies and subsidized domestic interest rates. These policies have encouraged the importation of sophisticated technology by making capital "too cheap" for both large-scale industrialists and commercial farmers. These policies have also perpetuated dualistic economies in which a large-scale, capital-intensive, modern sector coexists with a traditional, small-scale sector using labor-intensive methods (Brown 1979, 12–13). The remedy is to "get factor prices right"—that is, to permit market forces to determine the prices of capital and labor, so that they reflect their actual opportunity cost in that economy. In this formulation, land redistribution might be attempted, but the first priortiy is to correct the distortion in factor prices.

Proponents of redistributive land reforms acknowledge distortions in factor prices but see them as a consequence of the underlying inequalities in the distribution of land and other assets in the society. The distortions, they believe, are deliberately kept in place by pressure from politically and economically powerful groups that control most of the assets in a society and benefit unduly from cheap capital and protective tariffs. Redistributive measures such as land reform are repugnant to these groups.

Where politics is concerned, factor-price changes and redistributive strategies face similar problems. "Getting the prices right" can threaten strong vested interests, too. These two strategies are not incompatible and may be mutually reinforcing. In fact, the most frequently cited factor-pricing successes have occurred where agrarian structures are relatively egalitarian and land reforms have been implemented (Japan, Taiwan, South Korea, and Israel) (Brown 1979, 16–18). In a study of twelve Asian countries, Griffin and Ghose (1979) find no evidence of an agrarian crisis in Taiwan or South Korea, both of which had major land reforms. They suggest that an unequal distribution of income in rural areas is almost always associated with an unequal distribution of land, and that "measures to redistribute income should be regarded as complementary to a redistribution of wealth, not a substitute for it" (379).

Conclusion

This chapter has highlighted some of the major arguments and counterarguments of the past thirty to forty years about the socioeconomic issues and prospects of land reform. One caveat needs to be recorded, and it applies to all the theories and explanations offered, including those of the author: In the complex processes of development, and especially when these are treated at a global level, many causes interact to bring about consequences. Sometimes little is done analytically to disentangle these causes and assess their individual effects. There is an opportunity, says Long (1961), to "give full and free play to the analyst's perceptions and personal convictions, which often provide him with the major premise of his ultimate judgement" (114).

In the following chapter we examine the magnitude and the significance of the land reforms actually carried out in some of the Latin American countries.

3

Thirty Years of Reform:
Accomplishments and Limitations

Land reforms were carried out in a number of countries in several world regions in the late 1940s and the 1950s (Parsons et al 1956). Fundamental and successful reforms were completed in Japan, Taiwan, and South Korea. There were also major reforms in Egypt, Iraq, and Israel. Bolivian peasants in the early 1950s took possession of much of the land on the altiplano; their occupation of these lands was gradually legalized in the following decades. Mexico's reform movement, born of the 1910 revolution, enjoyed some resurgence in the 1950s and early 1960s. The Arbenz government in Guatemala distributed land to 100,000 families in 1953, only to have the process reversed by U.S.-backed counterrevolution (Chonchol 1989, 8). The Cuban revolution brought with it a basic land reform in the late 1950s. The reform that affected the most people and the most land was part of the Communist revolution on the Chinese mainland. Initial reforms in the early 1950s were followed by complete collectivization and communization of agriculture during the next two decades (Dorner and Thiesenhusen 1990).

In many of these cases the issues of agrarian reform had surfaced as a result of peasants' deep dissatisfaction with their economic position, which was often deplorable and deteriorating. All these reforms addressed fundamental political problems. The resolution of these problems would, of course, have major economic and social consequences as well. Many were seen, at least from a distance, as successful, or positive, achievements in development—especially in terms of social equity. This generally optimistic climate of opinion, the political dynamics of the Cold War, and the perspectives summarized in the previous chapter all helped shape the Kennedy administration's proposals leading to the Alliance for Progress. Increasing population growth and pressure on the land, the very high concentration of landownership, the need to stem the flow of rural migrants to the city, the prospects of land reform yielding not only greater equity but increased output and farm marketings as well—all were seen as providing incentives to implement reforms in the nations of Latin America (Dorner and Kanel 1971; Thiesenhusen 1989d).

Following the declaration of the Inter-American Economic and Social Council in 1961 that produced the Charter of Punta del Este establishing the Alliance for Progress, land reform legislation was passed in nineteen Latin American and Caribbean countries. Since then, national governments and international agencies have spent billions of dollars on land-related programs and projects throughout the region. Several kinds of effort have been initiated, including land reforms, land market intervention programs, and land settlement and colonization projects (Stringer 1989a, 1–2). U.S. assistance has provided some financial support for many of these undertakings.

Some Alliance-inspired legislation was designed specifically for settlement and colonization projects on public lands. For example, Costa Rica's Land and Settelement Law of 1961 established a special agency, the Instituto de Tierras Y Colonización (ITCO). This institute was transformed to the Instituto de Desarrollo Agrícola (IDA) in 1982 (Grau 1990, 219–20). Similar institutes or agencies were created in most countries to carry out land reform or colonization programs, either as autonomous entities or under ministries of agriculture, lands, or natural resources.

In practically all countries, legal concepts and instruments have changed over time. For example, in Chile, the 1962 law passed by the Alessandri administration established two new agencies: the Corporación de Reforma Agraria (CORA), which was charged with land acquisition and adjudication; and the Instituto de Desarrollo Agropecuário (INDAP), which was to provide credit and other services to reform beneficiaries. A 1967 law passed by the Frei Administration provided for a much more ambitious program of land acquisition under quick-taking procedures. This law also created an agrarian court system to resolve conflicts. The Allende government, from 1970 to 1973, used the same basic legal framework that had been established under the Frei government, but it greatly accelerated the pace of expropriation and reform. Other nations (for example, Ecuador, Peru, and the Dominican Republic) have had their own unique evolutionary patterns in both concept and substance of agrarian reform legislation.

What have been the outcomes of all these efforts? The fundamental problem in trying to answer this question is the near impossibility of isolating the consequences of reform efforts from the totality of dynamic forces driving change and development. Even in those very thorough reforms that have honored private property in land (for example, in Taiwan and South Korea), there is disagreement on the nature of the benefits received by the new landowners, the recipients (Apthorpe 1979; Powelson and Stock 1987). Also, different analysts using basically the same sources of secondary data come up with very different estimates of the number of beneficiaries and the amount of land affected. Some of these differences

Table 2.   Selected Countries of Latin America and the Caribbean: Land Reform
Beneficiaries

| Country | Thiesenhusen's Data[a] | | | Meyer's Data[b] | |
	Years	Percent of Farming Families Benefited	Forest and Agricultural Hectarage Affected	Years	Percent of Rural Households Benefiting
Bolivia	Up to 1977	74.5	83.4	1953–1975	78.9
Chile	Up to 1982	9.2	10.2	1962–1973	20.0
				1973–1975	4.0
Costa Rica	Up to 1980	5.4	7.1	1961–1979	13.5
Dominican Republic	1983 data	8.5	14.0	1962–1986	19.2
Ecuador	Up to 1983	10.4	9.0	1964–1976	9.1
Mexico	1970 data	42.9	43.4	1917–1980	52.4
Panama	1977 data	13.3	21.9	1963–1969	2.7
Peru	Up to 1982	30.4	39.3	1967–1979	21.3
Venezuela	Up to 1979	30.6	19.3	1959–1975	25.4

[a] Thiesenhusen (1989d, 10–11).
[b] Meyer (1989, 4).

might of course be the result of looking at different periods of a continuing
process (see Table 2).

There is another problem in speaking of the benefits and beneficiaries of
reform. In some cases, recipients of land did indeed gain status and economic advantage. But sometimes these gains were made at the expense of
even poorer landless families, who lost employment and wage-earning opportunities that were theirs previously. In other cases, the "beneficiaries"
received land but were then ignored and neglected, with the bulk of government and market services continuing to benefit the preexisting commercial
farmers.

Carrying a land reform through to a successful conclusion is extremely
complicated and difficult. It can be achieved only if there is a strong commitment and sufficient political will to counter the strong, often violent, opposition. In most of the nations of Latin America and the Caribbean, this kind of
firm and effective political will has been lacking. With the exceptions of the
Castro regime in Cuba and, more recently, the Sandinistas in Nicaragua, no
determined, reform-oriented government has remained in power for more
than a few years.

Political barriers are often reflected in reform legislation, not just overtly
obstructive legislation such as laws that prohibit organizing rural workers,
but also legal and administrative procedures that are established for the

explicit purpose of implementing land tenure reform. So long as people whose interests are threatened by reform hold power, they will find ways of assuring that legislation will be ineffective. The most frequent limitations of reform laws (see Dorner 1972, 30–31) include the following:

1. Lack of specific criteria for quick land-taking procedures, with resulting delays, litigation, and inaction
2. Requirements that all expropriated land be purchased with immediate cash payment at market prices, with ensuing financial restrictions confining any reform to relatively small areas
3. Primary emphasis on settlement in new areas, while the land tenure structure in presently productive areas (where most of the infrastructural investment exists) goes untouched
4. Complex and excessively legalistic procedures
5. Irregular and often inadequate financing in national budgets for agencies charged with implementing the reform
6. High retention limits for expropriated landowners

The Scope and Impact of Land Reforms in Latin America

This section draws heavily on the very comprehensive research review contained in Thiesenhusen's (1989d) edited volume, *Searching for Agrarian Reform in Latin America*.[1] Several countries not covered in this book will also be discussed, and in all cases, only a few highlights are presented. One must always keep in mind the great diversity between and within nations: all generalizations must be made with caution.

Ecuador

Four Ecuadorian land reform initiatives can be identified. First, the Agrarian Reform Law of 1964 was designed primarily to change the precapitalist labor relations in the Ecuadorian highlands. Peasants who had worked under very precarious conditions, some in the nature of "debt peonage," were to be given title to a plot of land of their own. Around 17,000 plots were so awarded. These averaged about 3.5 hectares in size, but the land was generally of lower quality than that worked by the beneficiaries prior to the reform.

A second reform ordered by a special 1970 decree was to apply primarily to the rice production areas of the lowlands. This, too, was to eliminate precapitalist labor relations, but the decree did not allocate land parcels;

1. For earlier reviews of the land tenure structures and attempts at reform, see Barraclough and Domike (1966) and Barraclough in collaboration with Collarte (1973).

instead, larger areas were expropriated, and production cooperatives were established. Again, the reform did not involve a significant amount of land, but it did contribute, as did the 1964 law, to the generalization of wage relations in agriculture.

A third agrarian reform law, passed in 1973, had the objective of achieving a measure of social justice along with sustained agricultural growth. A major focus was on expanding agricultural production. Increased state oil revenues were used to expand agricultural credit and technical assistance. In fact, however, the benefits accrued largely to medium and large producers. Very little expropriation occurred, and output growth was disappointing.

Finally, in 1977, special legislation was passed to encourage colonization in the Amazon region. By 1985, the reform sector in Ecuador represented nearly 30 percent of the total national farmland. However, over three-fourths of this was made up of colonization lands. While there were obviously some gains for peasants who had had no land before or had worked land under very precarious conditions, on balance, the medium and larger producers seem to have benefited the most from the several state interventions. The threat of state intervention, combined with greater access to official credit, encouraged large farmers either to modernize their farming operations or to sell land and pursue urban-industrial interests. Thus, the land reform legislation combined with market forces to change radically the traditional hacienda form of production organization. It is also most likely that some of these changes would have occurred without these specific government programs (Zevallos 1989, 42–69).

To illustrate the point about the diversity of conditions within a country, the Haneys (Haney and Haney 1989, 70–91) found major differences within the one province in the Central Highlands of Ecuador which was the focus of their study.[2] In Chimborazo, conditions varied greatly from north to south. Nonreform employment was relatively more important as an income source in the north. But the land reform measures were more relevant to those living in the central and southern regions of this province. Here too, however, the authors conclude that while the agrarian reform measures played an important role in altering the agrarian structure of Chimborazo, "many of the changes were already in progress when agrarian reform began" (Haney and Haney 1989, 85). "Inheritance patterns and land markets had begun to create a significant number of family-sized units before the agrarian reform" (76). Nevertheless, the Haneys, too, conclude that "those with larger farms—whether heirs who have modernized remnants of defunct haciendas or successful climbers—are clearly the major beneficiaries

2. For still another interesting dimension of the diversity, see the chapter by Forster (1989a), which presents a fascinating longitudinal study.

of the new agrarian structure, which still favors those who control the most productive resources" (87).

Peru

Although an agrarian reform law was passed in 1964, because of political opposition and major loopholes in the law, very little implementation followed. The government takeover by the military in 1968 was followed by new land reform legislation in 1969. This reform's basic objectives were "(1) to bring social justice to rural areas, (2) to support an enlargement of the internal market, and (3) to contribute to capital formation necessary for rapid industrialization" (Lastarria-Cornhiel 1989, 142). All farms over a certain size (which varied regionally) were, without exception, subject to expropriation. Most of the expropriated land was assigned to groups to be organized via several different forms of production cooperatives. As of September 1979, with the distribution virtually complete, 38.3 percent of the agricultural land as reported in the 1972 census had been redistributed to about 21 percent of all agricultural families (over 31 percent of families in need of land).

The results of this rather ambitious reform effort have been quite mixed. While the latifundio was largely eliminated and the power of the landed oligarchy reduced, the benefits of the reform have been quite uneven. Full-time permanent hacienda workers became part of the cooperative ownership, while the poorest seasonal workers and sharecroppers were usually excluded. Large-scale, modern sugar plantations on the coast were capital-rich compared to the poor, traditional haciendas in the highlands. Furthermore, many prereform peasant holdings were neglected by the reform process, and little was done to provide them with the required credit, inputs, and technical assistance they so badly needed.

There was also an urban bias in the government's macroeconomic policies. Capital was squeezed out of agriculture to subsidize industrialization. Price controls to keep food prices low in the cities discouraged production for the national market. Furthermore, the government underestimated the peasant's desire for individual ownership of land. The cooperatives were designed basically from the top down, without peasant input.

So, despite the rather far-reaching reforms implemented under the Velasco regime, beginning in 1981, Peruvian coastal agriculture underwent yet another transformation as the production cooperatives were subdivided into individual holdings. Each member of the cooperative typically received a 4–6 hectare parcel. By 1986, about three-fourths of the coastal production cooperatives had been parcelized (Carter and Alvarez 1989, 156).

Carter and Alvarez (1989) suggest that the longer-term viability of the new sector in terms of productivity and stability remains to be seen. "Is there an organizational alternative superior to both fully cooperative or fully parceled agriculture?" they ask. They conclude that "the seeming tragedy of restructuring Peruvian reform agriculture is that the remedy was postponed so long and was, because of beneficiary discontent, so radical. At the time of decollectivization, the CAPs [production cooperatives, or Cooperativas Agrarias de Producción], together with the 'cooperative movement,' lost legitimacy. Whether this loss is irreversible remains to be seen" (180).

Chile

Land reforms in Chile have occurred in three distinct phases: a land redistribution during the Frei administration (1964–70), an expanded and accelerated program during the Allende years (1970–73), and a reversal of the reform and the return of many of the reform lands to previous owners following the 1973 military coup. Under the Frei administration, nearly 3.5 million hectares were expropriated (including 280,000 hectares of irrigated land) and about 28,000 families received land.

The Frei reforms established the organizational form called the *asentamiento*. This was to be a temporary production-cooperative arrangement for three years, after which the recipients could choose the form of organization by majority vote. During this phase the day-to-day management was provided by an administrative committee elected by the members, under the supervision of Land Reform Agency personnel, who also provided technical and financial assistance.

The asentamiento has been criticized as merely replacing the former patron with the state agency and thus continuing the patron-client relationship of the prereform system. Another shortcoming of this form was that in general only the permanent estate workers were included as members. The poorest members of the rural society were hired as temporary wage workers as needed, much as the haciendas had done in the past (Thome 1989, 188–215). In fact, they may have hired fewer of such workers than under the old system because they "made room for their offspring and their *compadres* who had been expelled in the years of labor strife preceding the reform" (Brown 1989, 235).

The Popular Unity government of Salvador Allende expanded and accelerated the reforms begun by Frei. But increasing rural unrest and land invasions made it difficult to proceed with the reform in a planned and orderly fashion.

Land invasions were no longer aimed exlusively at haciendas: underpopulated *asentamientos* were increasingly targeted, often with the tacit support of factions within CORA [the agrarian reform corporation]. Radical Allendistas were challenging moderate Allendistas and Freistas to "reform the reform." . . . A second generation of reform was clearly gaining momentum in the latter part of Allende's administration—a fact that was not lost on counterreform elements that ultimately supported Pinochet's coup d'état. (Brown 1989, 236)

After the military coup in 1973, a conservative backlash led to a reversal of land reform policy. "Of the land originally expropriated, 57 percent (in terms of productive value) remained in the reform sector under cooperative or individual management, 28 percent was returned to previous owners, 5 percent was auctioned, and 10 percent was retained in the public sector" (Jarvis 1989, 245). Given the restrictive monetary and fiscal policies implemented by the Pinochet regime, many of the reform beneficiaries experienced severe economic problems. It is estimated that by 1986, about one-half of the 42,500 land reform beneficiaries had sold their land (Jarvis 1989, 249).

The belief that land reform had negative impacts on agricultural production was a major justification given by the military government for turning back the reform, yet there is no evidence to support this belief. "The rate of growth of agricultural value added during the 25 years prior to land reform, beginning in 1940, was 2.0 percent per year. . . . Since 1965, agriculture's average annual rate of growth was above this level except for 1972 and 1973" (Jarvis 1989, 265).

"On balance," concludes Brown, "the Chilean reform is better characterized as a modest (and flawed) success than as a failure" (Brown 1989, 237). He goes on to point out the achievements attributable to the reform: significant redistribution of wealth and income, changes in rural social relations, and advances in participatory development, among others. Unfortunately, the reform's long-run potential cannot be assessed since it was abruptly ended and to some extent reversed in 1973. Even so, it is altogether possible that the tenurial and other changes instituted and/or stimulated by the reform helped make subsequent macroeconomic policies more effective than they might otherwise have been.

Mexico

Mexico is in a league of its own with respect to Latin American land reforms. The constitution of 1917, preceded by years of bloody revolution which left one million dead, declared all land to be owned by the nation.

The state had the right to transmit this land to individuals in the form of private property, but always retained the right to expropriate the land whenever it was deemed necessary for public use. Yet, due to fragmented political forces following the revolution, major land redistribution did not take place until Cárdenas's rule in the 1930s. During the six years of the Cárdenas regime, almost 18 million hectares were distributed to 814,537 peasants. This exceeded the amount of land granted by all his predecessors.

In prior regimes distribution had been primarily of individual plots to each ejido member; however, faced with the need to expropriate large, irrigated haciendas while preserving the productivity of large units, Cárdenas created collective ejidos. Over time, however, most of these ejidos were decollectivized, with most of the land again being operated as individual small units.

The 1960s, under the presidency of Gustavo Díaz Ordaz, witnessed a large redistribution of land. About 25 million hectares (more than under Cárdenas) were distributed, but only about 10 percent of this land was arable. Furthermore, agricultural policies favored export promotion; this, combined with unfavorable internal terms of trade for agricultural products, led in the 1970s to sharp declines in the production of basic food crops along with dramatic increases in export crops, especially fruits and vegetables (Otero 1989, 276–304).

Currently, Mexico continues to have major difficulties in the rural areas—employment as well as productivity problems. Along with other Latin American nations, it suffers from the massive international debts accumulated in the 1970s and the economic depression of the 1980s. Mechanization and commercialization of agriculture combined with continuing rapid population growth create conditions of labor surplus which neither agriculture nor industry can fully absorb. But while the agrarian reform has not solved all the problems of the rural peasantry over the years, it has certainly provided new opportunities for millions and helped to ameliorate problems that otherwise might have been unmanageable.

Dominican Republic

In 1960 there were about 450,000 farmers in the Dominican Republic, and 1 percent of them owned over 50 percent of the land. After the thirty-year dictatorship of Rafael Trujillo, an agrarian reform law in 1962 created the Instituto Agrario Dominicano (IAD), whose task was to distribute state lands to individual farmers and provide them with the necessary technical assistance. During the 1960s, land concentration remained high, though a token reform sector grew slowly via the distribution of largely marginal farmlands. By 1972, political pressures from peasant organizations (with support in many instances from liberation-theology advocates associated with the Catholic Church), combined with the need for increased agricultural output, led to a more radical reform law. This and related laws provided for the expropriation of private lands (primarily rice lands over a given size). Roughly two-thirds of both land distributed and people benefited were realized in the ten years following passage of the 1972 law.

Individual assignments went to 32,275 reform beneficiaries in 267 settlements with an average of 5.3 hectares per recipient. There were 15,676 beneficiaries in 118 collectives with an average of 4.0 hectares per beneficiary. Currently, about one-third of the country's rice is produced by the reformed sector. "From the point of view of those who fashioned the agrarian laws of 1972, these efforts must be judged to be at least qualified successes" (Stanfield 1989, 334).

While the collective model was promoted to preserve economies of scale and to facilitate the delivery of inputs and services, several problems developed and grew in importance over time. First, the amount of payment received by an individual was not always conceived by other collective members to be commensurate with the amount of work such an individual performed (the free-rider problem). Second, the management of the collective by IAD was described by government as democratic, but in practice it tended to be authoritarian.

By the early 1980s, collective members expressed strong preferences for individual parcelization. A new law in 1985 permitted the creation of a modified organization known as the *associative asentamiento*. Individual plots of land are now assigned, providing the close link between effort and reward, while certain tasks and functions continue on a collective basis where clear economies exist, such as the contracting for credit and inputs and certain tillage and harvesting operations.

In the Dominican Republic, as in a number of other Latin American countries, the collective form of organization was temporary, yet it served an important interim function. Stanfield (1989) concludes that

> the experience with collectives strengthened the capabilities of reform beneficiaries to manage their own affairs and use their lands in a productive manner. The men and women who received access to land through the agrarian reform in the early 1970s are now different people. They have become, in large measure, managers and farmers—something that was almost impossible to imagine when the collectives were first organized. Indeed, these people seem to make up a new class in rural society. (334)

St. Lucia, Jamaica, and the Caribbean

The land tenure problems of the Caribbean region have their roots in the plantation system. Plantation owners' interests are fairly well protected by state property laws, but smallholders and the landless are much more vulnerable and insecure. The latter often seek to establish claims to the less productive land in the highlands on the periphery of the plantations. While St. Lucia and Jamaica differ in several critical ways, both have recently come to perceive smallholder tenure securtiy and related issues as high priorities. In both, the key land tenure issues are a highly skewed pattern of land distribution and family land.

Land fragmentation is leading to decreased parcel size as well as noncontiguous miniplots. Population pressure is certainly a factor, but it is not the only factor since, especially in Jamaica, urban migration and employment have provided alternative opportunities. Small property owners, however, are reluctant to sell their land when they migrate to the cities, since landownership confers both status and security. Instead, they rent out land to farmers who wish to increase their farm size, which leads those farmers to farm land fragments noncontiguous to the parcels they currently operate.

In Jamaica, the governments since the 1930s have focused on limited land acquisition for reallocation to landless farmers. Through 1985, 212 properties with a gross area of 202,262 acres provided 40,452 plots. For about one-half of these, secure land titles have been issued.

In both St. Lucia and Jamaica, as well as in other Caribbean island nations, family land creates special problems. *Family land* is land that may have claims against it by several generations of heirs. While the land may be operated by one or several individuals or families, siblings as well as previous and subsequent generational relatives of the operators may hold an undivided claim. Although there is a positive feature in that family-held land provides a counterforce to subdivision and fragmentation, this tenure form also creates many management problems.

Land cannot be sold without the consent of all those who hold an undivided claim to such land. Management decisions are complicated because produce, especially of perennial crops, may be subject to claims from these nonfarming, absentee owners. Steep hillsides, which should be in permanent tree crops, may be used for the cultivation of short-season or annual crops, leading to increased soil loss. Family lands also constrain credit use since they cannot ordinarly be used as collateral to secure loans.

A great deal of interest has been shown recently in the issuance of land titles. "The current generation of titling initiatives in the Caribbean will require careful monitoring. Only time will tell how productivity, investment and capitalization, distribution patterns, labor absorption in agriculture, subdivision rates and levels of fragmentation, credit access, farmer income levels, and the balance between food and export crops will be affected" (Bruce et al. 1989, 354).

Honduras

The agricultural sector in Honduras is characterized by a bipolar technological and social structure. A high-technology sector is dominated by bananas, and a low-technology subsistence sector produces corn, beans and other staples. It is estimated that over half of all farmers are squatters on public lands. Although land reform efforts have been ongoing since 1962, and reform has been cited as one of the top priorities of the government in recent development plans, results have been quite limited. The reformed sector includes only about 8 percent of the nation's farmland and 10 percent of rural families. The majority of the land redistributed was public or state lands, often of marginal quality. This, along with limited services, has undoubtedly contributed to the fact that by 1985, over one-fifth of the beneficiaries had deserted their land.

Despite the limited impact of land reform efforts, the struggle of peasant organizations has given these groups an unusually influential role in the formulation of agrarian policies. Three national *campesino* associations are among the best organized in Latin America. These organizations benefited from leaders who had gained experience during the banana strikes of 1954. Success achieved by way of these strikes provided confidence and recognition of the advantages to be gained through collective action in the face of politically powerful companies and the government. A variety of tactics has been used—land invasions, protest marches—to pressure the government to act in their behalf. "Although not always successful, they have been responsible for acquiring thousands of manzanas of land (1 manzana = 1.75 acres), for the dismissal of three INA [National Agrarian Institute] directors, for electing one of their officers to Congress, and for obtaining key appointments on the National Agrarian Council" (Stringer 1989b, 370). Nevertheless, although the reform has made a positive difference in the lives of many rural families, it remains of limited scope.

Nicaragua

When the Sandinistas came to power in 1979, they soon took over the landholdings of former dictator Somoza and his close associates, which comprised about one-fifth of Nicaragua's arable land. The government's concern with maintaing production and the benefits of scale economies on these large, modern estates (along with the fear that parcelization for individualized farming would reduce the production of export crops) led to the decision to manage these confiscated holdings as state farms. This effort came under the administration of the Nicaraguan Agrarian Reform Institute, a special agency established in July 1979.

In a second phase of the reform, authorized under the Agrarian Reform

Law of 1981, "landowners with over 350 hectares in the Pacific regions or over 700 hectares in the central regions could have their lands expropriated for underutilization, sharecropping, or disinvestment, or if areas were declared to be agrarian reform zones" (Kaimowitz 1989, 386). According to the law, the postreform organization could take the form of state farms, production cooperatives, or individualized farming. Beginning in 1983, agricultural policy came to favor production cooperatives for the postreform organizational structure.

Beginning in 1984, a major focus of the reform was the granting of property titles to squatters. Almost 30,000 families received titles between 1984 and 1985. By 1986, the minimum holding size subject to expropriation was lowered, making further distribution possible. More attention was also given to assuring that individual producers received the needed technical assistance. Like other policies since 1982, these measures favored the people living in areas of military conflict. While agricultural performance generally was quite satisfactory up until 1984, military conflict and increasing foreign exchange difficulties led to a decline in agricultural output after 1984. At about this time, because of both the military conflict and the improved administration, a decentralization and regionalization of reform-policy implementation was instituted. This resulted in increased local participation as well as better adaptation of policies to local conditions. For example, "the Atlantic coast agrarian reform process is sharply different from that in the Pacific area. It places a premium on the titling of lands to indigenous communities and not on organizing cooperatives or individuals" (Kaimowitz 1989, 405).

While the Sandinistas, at least in the initial years, tended to view the peasants as a "proletariat in formation," one which should be encouraged to organize for proletarian interests, the peasant farmers of the north and central regions and the "semiproletarians of the Pacific region" saw themselves as farmers, not as wage workers. As the complexity of the agrarian structure and the perspectives of the peasant producers became better understood, policies became more flexible and pragmatic. This was reflected in the authorization of a special peasant-farmer organization to represent producers not willing to join the rural workers association (Reinhardt 1989, 465). Despite some confusions and setbacks and the constant military threat of the Contras, Reinhardt (1989, 476) estimates that 55 percent of the rural poor have received land under these reforms. It has been one of the most wide-reaching land reforms in Latin America.

El Salvador

The agrarian reform in El Salvador began in 1980 and consists of three major phases. First, estates over 500 hectares were expropriated, with owners retaining 100–150 hectares (the larger exemption applying in areas of poorer soil quality). The expropriated area was farmed by groups of farmers organized into production cooperatives which were co-managed by the government. Phase two was to have provided for the expropriation of landholdings over 100 (but less than 500) hectares. This, however, has been postponed. The Constitution of 1983 essentially made this part of the law inoperable. It increased the area a landowner could retain to 245 hectares, it allowed the landowner to choose the location of the land to be retained, and it gave owners two years to transfer the excess areas voluntarily to other farmers (transfer to family members was specifically prohibited). The final phase was a land-to-the-tiller provision whereby "tenants and sharecroppers could file claims and become owners of whatever small plots they rented in March 1980, up to 10 manzanas (7 hectares) in total" (Strasma 1989, 410). It is estimated that approximately 22 percent of the rural poor have benefited from these reforms (involving perhaps an equal proportion of the nation's farmland) (Diskin 1989, 443).

As with reforms in several of the other Latin American countries, the production cooperatives have been criticized for benefiting the full-time workers while excluding the poorest, landless workers. Many cooperatives prefer not to utilize all their land (and used hired labor) rather than admit more new members. Some members tend to respond to options within the cooperative structure as workers would on state farms rather than as co-owners of the enterprise. The co-management by sometimes incompetent government technicians provides the rationale for such behavior. There is no policy for graduation of the cooperatives to self-management, and the free-rider problem continues to plague the cooperatives. A high level of debt and inadequate state services (credit, inputs, technical assistance) have also been obstacles for the development and maturation of these cooperatives (Strasma 1989, 419).

The potential beneficiaries under the land-to-the-tiller program experienced many problems with an extremely complicated procedure involved in obtaining land under this phase. Delays in implementation, political changes, and a lack of communication with the peasantry left many unable and unwilling to file a claim against their landlord. This is understandable given the fact that many of the potential beneficiaries were illegally evicted (Diskin 1989, 439). Even those who followed these complicated procedures have experienced difficulties after having their claim vindicated. They found themselves paying a mortgage on a small (average of 3.8 acres) parcel of land of questionable quality. "A sample survey of Phase III households found that net income from Phase III parcels accounted for about one-third of the families' total net annual income" (Reinhardt 1989, 469).

While a sizable proportion of families eligible did receive land and new opportunities under the reforms, the effort can also be criticized as being too little, too late, and too constricted. "For the rural poor in El Salvador, most of whom received no benefit, agrarian reform remains a distant goal, one yet to be achieved" (Diskin 1989, 447).

Colombia

Colombia had experienced over a decade (1948 to 1960) of what was referred to as *la violencia*—basically a civil war. This long period of serious unrest and violence in the countryside, as well as the Cuban revolution, which frightened the large landowners, along with the encouragement offered by the Alliance for Progress convinced the Colombian government to change its agrarian policy. In 1961, the Colombian Congress passed Law 135, which provided for agrarian reform. This was to include land titling, colonization on public lands, provision of rural services, and authority to expropriate and parcelize private land (Felstehausen 1971; Boer et al. 1985).

In the first period of the reform (1962–67,) very little land was expropriated. The agrarian reform agency (Instituto Colombiano de la Reforma Agraria, INCORA) emphasized the granting of titles to small farmers on public lands. In the second phase (1968–72), a more active and radical program was undertaken. A peasant association emerged, the Asociación Nacional de Usuarios Campesinos (ANUC), and hundreds of farms were invaded. Almost 200,000 hectares were incorporated under INCORA's management, and collective farms were established.

But the agrarian reform remained a marginal one. In fact, the distribution of land was more unequal in 1970 than in 1960 (Boer et al. 1985, 114). In the early 1970s, the strategy shifted to focus on integrated rural development, and the idea of land redistribution was essentially abandoned. After 1973, the third and continuing period, "INCORA was . . . consolidating . . . results of the first two periods and was hindered by a yearly decreasing budget in real terms. As a result, [as of] 1978 only 1.6 percent of the cultivated land was redistributed to 27,568 families" (Boer et al. 1985, 114).

Paraguay

Very little land reform had been carried out in Paraguay under the thirty-plus years of the Stroessner dictatorship, but the new government which took over after Stroessner was deposed is debating the options.[3] Colonization on public lands was the main vehicle of reform throughout the 1960s

3. Information for this section was obtained during a ten-day consulting mission in December 1989.

and 1970s. In the 1980s, however, the supply of public lands suitable for agriculture and available for accommodating peasant pressures ran out. Meanwhile, unemployment rose dramatically following completion of a major dam-construction project on the eastern edge of the country. The economic recession in Paraguay as well as in the neighboring countries of Argentina and Brazil simultaneously closed many of the job options that had existed in the 1970s. A variety of campesino leagues and organizations came into being, some supported by urban groups and the Catholic Church. A surge of land invasions arose in the eastern provinces in the late 1980s. A land reform policy is under serious discussion by government agencies.

Venezuela

Peasant organizations played an important role in Venezuela's agrarian reforms. In 1945, the Democratic Action (AD) party came to power. Peasant unionization was promoted, and in 1948 a land reform law was enacted. However, it was not implemented because the AD government was replaced by the conservative regime of Pérez Jimenez following a reactionary military coup. Over the next ten years, the National Peasant Federation was suppressed. Many of the leaders were imprisoned for varying lengths of time and were then exiled. While a substantial agrarian reform was carried out under the AD from 1945 to 1948, "by the end of the Pérez Jimenez dictatorship almost all the land that had been used for agrarian reform under AD from 1945–1948 had come under private control, and almost all of the peasants formerly settled thereon had been evicted" (Powell 1971, 94).

In 1958, the Jimenez regime was overthrown, and the AD returned to power. The peasant movement soon reorganized as leaders returned from exile and others emerged from underground. The first Peasant Congress was convened in Caracas in June 1959. The atmosphere was militant and aggressive. There was, in fact, a growing apart of factions within this peasant movement: some wanted to push for more land invasions and militate for a more rapid and drastic reform (this could threaten the reformist government by strengthening the opponents of the right); some wished to cooperate with the new government in resolving administrative problems of the reform in hopes of enhancing the long-term prospects of success and minimizing political opposition to reform (this could alienate the loyalty of the militant elements among the peasant masses). The major factions opted for government cooperation. Nevertheless, in addition to the very productive role of the cooperating campesino organizations, the militants also went forward with more land invasions and other aggressive actions (Powell 1971, 103–106).

In 1960, a new agrarian reform law was passed. The agrarian reform that followed did expropriate a fair amount of private lands, but Venezuela's oil wealth, perhaps unique among Latin American countries, permitted a handsome compensation to be paid to landowners whose estates were expropriated. Venezuela also had a large amount of public lands suitable for farming on its inland southern frontier. Thus, almost three-fourths of all lands taken for redistribution came from the public domain. By the middle to late-1970s, over 8 million hectares of land had been distributed to 150,000 families (over 35 percent of all rural families). Less than half of these families had clear title to their lands at that time. Some 30 percent had provisional titles and others continued as "occupants" of land controlled by the National Agrarian Institute (IAN) (World Bank 1978; Venezuela 1979).

Brazil

While land reform has entered the political debate in Brazil (Carter and Mesbah 1990, 1), there is little evidence of land reform activity in that country. The 1940-through-1980 census data indicate that land distribution is becoming ever more concentrated. The Gini coefficient was .825 in 1940 and .853 in 1980 (Thiesenhusen and Melmed-Sanjak 1990, 396). The Amazon frontier continues to act as a safety valve by relieving social and political pressure. This movement into the Amazon may also jeopardize Brazil's long-run economic future, because it threatens the global ecosystem itself. Yet to date, Brazil has not really confronted its land-tenure problems within the settled areas of the country (Thiesenhusen and Melmed-Sanjak 1990, 396).

Government policies treat land as a very abundant factor. There is a large (in terms of numbers of people), labor-absorptive small-farm sector producting substantial amounts of agricultural output with relatively meager amounts of capital, but land availability to this sector is declining. In addition the major thrusts of government policy tend to support large, extensive production and ownership units and discriminate against the small farmer.

> For example, Binswanger (1987) argues that land is wastefully used partially because income-tax laws virtually exempt agriculture, thus converting it into a tax shelter. Especially at the frontier, urban investors and corporations are competing vigorously for land to establish livestock ranches, he claims. But tax treatment even makes it attractive for wealthy individuals to buy land from small farmers in areas of well-established settlement. Large farms are able to profit because they receive subsidized credit and utilize it well. (Thiesenhusen and Melmed-Sanjak 1990, 408)

But we should also remember that Brazil is a very large land mass and is most diverse in terms of its ecological zones as well as its land tenure structures. Thiesenhusen and Melmed-Sanjak (1990) conclude that "the

Northeast appears to be primarily bimodal, the emergent capitalized family farm seems to be crucial to understanding the South, and the large farm is preeminent on the frontier" (408).

Bolivia

In Bolivia, some traditional landholdings were broken up and sold to peasants before the 1952 revolution. These were in most cases in a few of the smaller villages, where landholdings were smaller and population pressure was particularly high; in general, landlord associations exerted pressure to prevent individual landlords from selling or renting lands to peasants. Land concentration in the country was extreme, with 92 percent of all land in farms held in units of 1,000 hectares or larger while 82 percent of all owners controlled a mere 1 percent of the land. The pre-1952 period in large areas of the country was marked by land invasions, violence, and conflict between peasants and landlords. In 1953, the new government of the Revolutionary Movement party promulgated a land reform decree. The basic objective of the reform was to transform the feudalistic land tenure system by promoting a more equitable distribution of land, increasing productivity of land and labor, and integrating peasants into the national economy and society (Clark 1971; World Bank 1978).

Initially some of the lands that were invaded and taken over by the campesinos were organized into peasant syndicate production cooperatives. By the early 1970s, however, almost all such lands had been distributed in individual parcels. Land redistribution was rapid in most areas (and most of it was accomplished by campesinos themselves rather than by government under the land reform decree) and was largely complete by 1955. Although about half of Bolivia's rural families had become farm owner-operators, the certification of land titles was drawn out over the next three decades.

Throughout the postwar period, colonization of unsettled lands received considerable support from the Bolivian government and foreign lending institutions, but spontaneous migration and settlement had by far the greatest impact. The land reform process per se had its largest impact on the prerevolutionary croplands. Only about 10 percent of croplands remain in the very large units that were common before the reform. On the other hand, livestock ranches in the mountainous parts of Bolivia were relatively untouched (or were established after the reforms). Thus, nearly two-thirds of the nation's farmland (cropland and rangeland combined) is still in holings of over 1,000 hectares (World Bank 1978, 21–23). The government was also unable to provide many of the services that reform beneficiaries required, due primarily to very limited resources. Nevertheless, "The Bolivian Revolution, the land reform, and the peasant organizations led to a considerable degree of integration of the masses of peasants into the national economy, society, and policy" (Clark 1971, 159).

Concluding Commentary on the Scope and Impact of Land Reform

As documented in the individual country experiences, a number of significant changes have taken place which are not related to land reform, or are only indirectly related. Very large holdings have been broken up via expropriation or "voluntary" divestment. Agriculture in general has come under the direction of more entrepreneurial-minded owners and managers as contrasted to the more traditional style prevailing before the 1960s. A very significant investment and capitalization process has occurred. In many cases the traditional hacienda permanent work force (or *service tenants*) has been sharply reduced as a result of mechanization, while demand for part-time seasonal workers has increased. While there are many among the peasantry who are downwardly mobile, there are also some who have become upwardly mobile without any help from agrarian reform. Finally, all countries have become much more urbanized, and a combination of import-substitution and export-promotion policies has provided major impetus to increased urban employment.

Economic trends that have been much more directly affected by the reforms include the voluntary division of some large holdings into medium-sized, capital-intensive farms. Likewise, the number of less capitalized, small family units has increased substantially in some countries as a result of land provided directly in small units or as a result of the decollectivization of recent years. A direct result of the reforms has been to make the peasantry more heterogeneous. While these have been positive results of the reforms, some negative consequences must also be recognized. In most cases reforms were quite partial, and land was often granted to those among the peasantry who were among the better-off rather than those in the deepest poverty. Likewise, in some cases the services crucial to a productive agriculture—inputs, credit, markets— were not available via the private sector and were not supplied by government, leading to land abandonment by a substantial number of the beneficiaries (Thiesenhusen 1989b, 483–501).

Peasant Organizations and Production Cooperatives

In discussions of the various country experiences, the role of peasant organizations has surfaced on a number of occasions. Likewise, production cooperatives and other forms of group farming have been a part of a number of the Latin American land reforms. Both of these forms of organization can, and in some instances have, played a key role in land reforms.

At times peasant movements have been instigated and fostered by peasants themselves; at other times they have been primarily the creations of urban intellectuals and politicians (Brown 1971). In the case of peasant organizations, one needs to distinguish between those whose origins and purposes are found in the struggle for land and fighting for peasants' rights, and those created primarily to perform economic functions.

Peasant collective action in the fight for land was more significant in the early reforms—those of Mexico, Bolivia, and Venezuela. However, there were certainly active peasant organizations which made a difference in the Honduran reforms and, to a lesser extent, in the Dominican Republic and El Salvador. The main thrust of peasant collective action has been land invasions as a means of pressuring the government or simply as a means of defying the government's inaction. At times governments responded positively to meet some of the invaders' demands for land; at other times such initiatives were crushed with military force. Such was the case with the organization in southern Peru called La Convención y Lares, which invaded land in the late 1950s. While it had seized the land and gained control over the area, the army was eventually called in to restore order and remove the invaders (Lastarria-Cornhiel 1989, 136).

In general, the efforts of peasant organizations in Latin America were primarily attempts to gain political power and/or to convince those in power to lend a helping hand in satisfying peasant demands for land and a better life. Rarely were these organizations created to serve economic functions such as joint efforts directed at obtaining credit, marketing products, or purchasing inputs and supplies. The landless, of course, had little use for such economic cooperatives, but even those with some land (who did need inputs, credit, and market outlets) rarely organized for these purposes. In part at least, this reluctance or inability to organize for the pursuit of economic interests is a direct consequence of the bimodal structure of landholding, where input, output, credit, and marketing channels are all geared to serving the large producers. Even after land redistribution, effective economic organizations of this nature have been difficult to establish.

This political focus of Latin American peasant organizations stands in sharp contrast to that of farmer organizations in the East Asian reforms. For example, a most fortuitous asset available to those implementing the agrarian reforms in Taiwan was the existence of farmers' associations. These associations were created and promoted by the Japanese colonial government at the turn of the century. After changes and consolidations under both the Japanese and later the Chinese government, the control of these farmers' associations has come to rest entirely with the farmers since the reorganization of 1953. These associations were critical partners with government in promoting agricultural research, extension services, farm credit, input and product marketing, and the like. Today, these farmers' associations in Taiwan are a federated system of multipurpose cooperative organizations working to promote the interests of agricultural producers and the welfare of the entire rural community and economy (Lin, Shih-Tung 1990, 163; Dorner and Thiesenhusen 1990).

There have, of course, been postreform efforts in a number of Latin American countries to assist in creating economically based peasant organizations. In some cases the preexisting, politically oriented peasant unions were used as the basis for new groups with economic functions. In other cases special groups were established, which were often organized during land reform into production cooperatives.

However, production cooperatives or collectives have been reorganized in many countries that established this form, with about the only exception being Cuba. They continue with varying degrees of prominence in Honduras, Nicaragua, and El Salvador. In Mexico, most production on ejido lands comes from individual plots (Dovring 1969, 2). In Chile, as noted earlier, the asentamientos were gradually converted into individual plots under the military government, which strongly favored individual property (Jarvis 1989). Even without this governmental effort, it is likely that asentamiento members would have chosen the privatization route. Some asentamientos did mature during the Frei administration, and it is worth noting that most chose a mixed system, preserving economies of scale in the collective organization of orchards, vineyards, and pastures while dividing the land for individual operation in the production of cereals and truck crops (Brown 1989, 223). Similar trends in the breakup of cooperatives are evident in Peru (Melmed 1988) and the Dominican Republic (Stringer et al. 1985).

Why then were these collective forms of organization chosen? What problems led to their demise? In some cases, presumably, production cooperatives were established for ideological reasons. Elsewhere, it seemed impractical to establish a larger number of small-scale, individual farms in a short period of time. Also, in some large-scale production units, a considerable amount of capital investment existed that was either indivisible (large machinery, stables, irrigation systems) or required time and new investment to make it serve many small units. Brown (1989) reasons as follows in the case of Chile: "*Asentamientos* and other production cooperatives are not much in favor these days, and few would argue that they represent a viable long-term alternative. But their value as a transitional form in a market-oriented economy has probably been underestimated" (237). One might add that the asentamiento also provided time for people who had been farm laborers—not managers and entrepreneurs—to gain some experience in directing a farm enterprise. Furthermore, in some cases, the production cooperative actually extended benefits of the reform to the excluded. Carter and Alvarez (1989) note that the production-cooperative system is often criticized for benefiting only the "privileged stratum of the 'upper poor' . . . [in Peru]. The intrinsic labor problems of the CAP model inadvertently extended second-class reform benefits to the many individuals hired as full-time wage laborers, or 'permanent-temporary' workers as they became known" (172).

Collective forms of agriculture are now being abandoned in many parts of the world. The People's Republic of China has established the production-responsibility system and has essentially returned to individual farming. Decollectivization is gaining momentum in East European countries, and the Soviet Union itself is experimenting with modified forms. Why is this trend so pervasive? For one thing, the people of the collectives (the member-participants) were seldom consulted as to what they thought and what they wanted. Peasants the world over wish to have land of their own. What's more, there are serious operational and managerial problems in production collectives. In a survey conducted in the Dominican Republic (Stringer et al. 1985), the reasons given for division of land and privatization of operations were as follows:

1. We get the same percentage of the net income if we work hard or if we don't work at all.
2. We see that some crops are planted and cultivated on time and others not. When we control planting and weeding, we do it right.
3. We never see the bookkeeping; we know neither costs of production nor total production. The check we got at the end of the year was always much lower than we expected, and the income we received was much inferior to what we earn now.
4. We can't keep our family working because no place is allowed for them to be paid wages.
5. We can't pass unencumbered land on to our children after our death.
    The complaints thus seemed to be directed not against the collective as such, but against the way the rules were designed and the seemingly arbitrary and rigid, almost capricious, manner in which they were carried out. (18)

One of the key problems in collective agriculture is trying to get a close match between individual effort expended and the rate of compensation. The Chinese used a system of work points, but it basically measured and reflected time spent rather than work performed. There is always the free-rider problem. Yet any attempt at basing work points on specific tasks completed, rather than points per workday (in accordance with the worker's age, physical strength, special skills, and so forth), would also be difficult. It would involve a costly and time-consuming cataloguing of thousands of distinct tasks and vast expenditures of supervisory and accounting effort (Putterman 1985, 70). In the case of the family farm or self-employment, this monitoring problem does not exist, because the connection between effort and return requires no measurement or disbursement procedure. In the group enterprise, with its joint inputs of labor and other factors, it is no longer possible to identify the physical product of an individual's contribution (Putterman 1987, 117).

Nolan (1983) has put the problem well:

> Agriculture has peculiar diseconomies of scale because of the special problems of supervising farm labor. Its sequential nature, with tasks altering during the agricultural cycle, limits the possibilities for the division of labour; dispersed activity over a wide area inhibits labour control; lack of uniformity of natural resources makes work-norm estimation difficult; and the temporal separation of labour inputs from its results, as well as the hazards of climate, pests, etc., causes difficulties in calculating its overall contribution to the final product. (386)

The cooperative form of organization in agriculture is very complex. Even with supportive efforts by government agencies, problems of effective internal organization and of member commitment and morale will arise in group farming. It is a delusion to expect that group farms have such obvious benefits to members, or such decisive economic advantages, that organizational problems are easily overcome. These organizational problems arise largely because of ambiguities in the roles of both managers and members of group farms. Members are supposed to be both workers and participants in policymaking; managers are supposed to supervise the workers and at the same time be responsible to them. A common outcome of this dilemma is ineffective management on the one hand and poor work discipline and absence of effective participation in policymaking by the members on the other. This result has been called a *we-they system*, in which there is mutual suspicion between members and managers, and in which members have little or no identification with or control over the organization (Dorner and Kanel 1977). "The specific problem with CAPs," conclude Carter and Alvarez (1989), "lies in the difficulty which CAPs have in generating *authority* . . . to enforce . . . ample work for the tasks at hand" (170).

As indicated by the respondents in the Dominican Republic survey, one of the key problems with production cooperatives is the lack of accountability of management. This is a critical flaw in an organization where compensation of labor is apparently based on year-end net earnings of the enterprise. This is one of the fundamental differences between the production cooperative and the large private estate or even the state farm. Under either of the latter two organizational forms, there is some type of wage contract which must be honored irrespective of profits. Wages are not contingent upon year-end economic results of the enterprise. In the case of state farms, there is a clear separation between the managers and the labor force. Quick decisions are possible and can be taken without the problems associated with the participation of large numbers of workers/co-owners. Yet state farms have all the other weaknesses of eliciting full commitment of the labor force and labor supersvision. Thus, not many state farms continue to exist. Large private estate operation, when they become more commercialized and capitalized, turn to mechanization and operating with a reduced, more specialized work force.

There is one seeming exception to this problem of the difficulties inherent in the supervision of a large labor force in a large-scale, diversified farming operation: the modern plantation. But one of the key differences of the plantation is its highly specialized production (usually only one product—sugar, bananas, tea, cocoa, and the like). Work is also more specialized and has some features of the factory in manufacturing. There is ordinarily a need for close coordination between harvesting and shipping or processing of plantation crops. If sugarcane is left unprocessed for more than twelve hours, it loses sugar content to fermentation. Fairly mature bananas must be on a refrigerated ship or plane within twenty-four hours of harvest to delay further ripening. On the other hand, wheat and rice can be easily stored and milled any time throughout the year (Binswanger and Elgin 1990).

The production cooperative form of organization in agriculture has had its share of problems, as noted in the several cases above. But one should not conclude from this that all manner and means of cooperation are likewise subject to these same problems. Cooperative efforts among and between farmers are vital. This applies not only to cooperative activities for buying inputs, selling outputs, and obtaining credit, but also to certain production functions as well; we need to recognize that there are many different levels of cooperation.

One typology of agricultural collectivism (Reed 1977, 1978) noted differences in function in moving from the least to the most integrated forms of agricultural cooperation:

1. Joint operations: A group cooperates in a single operation or task. Land and capital may be privately owned but are pooled for a specific

task, and individuals are paid according to the amount of labor and capital provided.

2. Joint farming: Much the same as joint operations, except that pooling of resources and joint operations center on at least one farm enterprise operated in common.

3. Cooperative farming: A more integrated form that includes collective operation of most enterprises. Land and capital are cooperatively managed, though individuals may have the right to withdraw property they had contributed to the joint enterprise. Payments are made to labor according to the amount of work performed, and payments for land and capital are made in accordance with the amounts that individuals contributed to the cooperative farming venture.

4. Collective farming: All enterprises are operated collectively. Land and capital are owned collectively. Payments are made for labor contributions only, with no payment for land or capital that individual members may have contributed.

5. Commune: All enterprises are operated collectively. All productive land and capital as well as housing is held communally. Distribution is according to need, with a high level of collective consumption.

It is evident that agricultural cooperatives include a diverse set of possible arrangements. Some of this diversity may appear in the same form of collective operating in different social, cultural, political, and economic contexts. The key dimensions in which these differences seem to exist are ownership of resources (in some cases the government rather than individuals or the cooperative owns the land); socialization of work, including both physical labor and management; access of members to decision-making processes and the means by which managers are chosen and kept accountable to the members; distribution of output; and degree of socialization of consumption.

Evaluation and Conclusions

This overview of Latin American land reforms over the past thirty years allows no clear and definitive judgment about these efforts. Compared to the East Asian reforms (Japan, Taiwan, South Korea), those of Latin America were of a different order. At least in hindsight, this is not surprising. The political will in the East Asian reforms was not provided by an internal government with close ties to the landed classes. It was, in contrast, provided by outside powers with virtually no ties to the landed classes. It is also clear that the hopes and expectations raised by the Alliance for Progress were not realized.

One might raise hypothetical and unanswerable questions: Would conditions be better, would there be fewer poor families, would there be greater equity and greater output if there had been no efforts at reform? One can only speculate, but this seems highly doubtful. Would conditions be much different if the reforms had been carried through as thoroughly as they were in the East Asian countries? The answer would obviously be in the affirmative if this had been possible. But the original conditions (the bimodal structure in Latin America versus the unimodal structure in Asia) were so different that the situations are not comparable.

There were certainly many obstacles preventing better performance in Latin America: settlements located in remote areas, poor land not well suited to farming, lack of inputs and other services, lack of appropriate infrastructure, too little land per family, inflexible tenure systems, poor management and bureaucratic top-down controls, and so forth. These shortcomings, it must be emphasized, are not inherent to land reform as a public policy. Rather, they reflect a lack of commitment and effective political will and, at times, of course, an insufficiency of resources for adequate implementation. These factors provide little confidence that future efforts would be much better; however, every future case must be judged on its own potential merits.

4

Prospects for the 1990s:
Are Reforms Still Needed?

Basic Structural Changes Since 1960

In a region as diverse as Latin America, most generalizations about socioeconmonic trends or policies are likely to be wrong in
many particulars. It seems more or less accurate to say, however, that many
socioeconomic indicators show positive advancement. While the 1960s and
1970s were decades of fairly rapid economic growth, the accumulation of
massive debts in the late 1970s and early 1980s, along with a general recession in the latter period, resulted in relative stagnation through the first half
of the 1980s, especially in the industrial sector (see Table 3).

From the 1960s to the present, there have been some significant changes
in the population structure. Population growth continued at fairly high
rates, but there is evidence of a leveling off in most areas. There has been
spectacular growth in urban populations. Of great significance is the fact
that in 1960, the rural population was growing in all countries, but by the
mid-1980s, a substantial number of countries show stability or even decline
in absolute numbers of rural people (see Table 4).

The last column in Table 4 (column 9) shows the annual percentage by
which the urban population would have to grow in order to have a constant
or declining rural population. This rate should be compared to that in column 8. If the rate shown in column 8 is greater than that in column 9, then
the rural population should be declining in absolute terms (shown by a
negative value in column 7). According to this comparison, about thirteen
countries (including the United States) have a declining rural population (or
the rural population has about stabilized; examples include Chile, Colombia, Argentina, and the Dominican Republic). Nine countries continue to
have growing rural populations.[1]

---

1. Some caution needs to be exercised with these comparisons. The data on urbanization
may be particularly vulnerable to misinterpretation. The World Bank (1988) offers the following caveat: "Because the estimates in this table are based on different national definitions of
what is *urban*, cross-country comparisons should be interpreted with caution. Data on urban

Table 3.   Some Indicators of Socioeconomic Changes in Selected Countries of Latin
America and the Eastern Caribbean (with the United States for comparison)

Country	Agriculture (average annual growth rates)		Industry (average annual growth rates)		Infant Mortality (per 1,000 live births)	
	1965–80	1980–86	1965–80	1980–86	1965	1986
Argentina	1.4%	2.3%	3.3%	−1.7%	58	33
Bolivia	3.8	−1.8	3.7	−7.5	160	113
Brazil	3.8	2.0	9.9	1.6	104	65
Chile	1.6	3.1	0.8	0.7	107	20
Colombia	4.3	2.3	5.5	3.8	96	47
Costa Rica	4.2	2.2	8.7	1.1	72	18
Cuba	N.R.	N.R.	N.R.	N.R.	38	14
Dominican Republic	4.6	1.0	10.9	1.0	110	67
Ecuador	3.4	1.0	13.7	3.5	112	64
El Salvador	3.6	−2.3	5.3	−0.7	120	61
Guatemala	5.1	−0.4	7.3	−3.0	112	61
Haiti	1.0	−1.3	7.1	−2.4	178	119
Honduras	1.6	2.2	5.7	−0.8	128	72
Jamaica	0.5	1.4	−0.1	−1.3	49	19
Mexico	3.2	2.1	7.6	−0.1	82	48
Nicaragua	3.3	1.4	4.2	0.3	121	65
Panama	2.4	2.2	5.9	−1.4	56	24
Paraguay	4.9	1.9	9.1	−0.7	73	43
Peru	1.0	2.2	4.4	−1.1	130	90
Uruguay	1.0	−0.7	3.1	−5.2	48	28
Venezuela	3.9	2.3	3.4	−0.8	65	37
United States	1.1	3.1	1.9	3.2	25	10

Source: World Bank 1988.
N.R. = no response.

If opportunities in the cities were plentiful and sufficient to absorb
off-farm migrants, one might conclude that a declining farm population
signifies at least the potential for a rising standard of living for city and
country folks alike. Historical experience confirms that a country's living
standard, as measured by average per-capita income, increases as the
share of the population required for the production of food declines. Fur-

population are from population censuses, which are conducted at only five or even ten-year
intervals" (304). Also, the calculations in columns 6, 7, and 9 of Table 4 are approximations.

Table 4.   Changes in Population and Population Structure in Selected Countries of Latin America and the Eastern Caribbean (with the United States for comparison)

Country	Total Population Growth Rates 1965–80 (1)	Total Population Growth Rates 1980–86 (2)	Numbers (in millions) 1986 (3)	Proportion of Total Population That Is Urban 1965 (4)	Proportion of Total Population That Is Urban 1985 (5)	Total Population That Is Urban[a] (in millions) 1985 (6)	Population Growth Rates 1980–85 Rural[b] (7)	Population Growth Rates 1980–85 Urban (8)	Urban Population Growth Rate Needed to Stabilize or Reduce Rural Population[c] (9)
Argentina	1.6%	1.6%	31	76%	84%	26	+.04%	1.9%	1.91%
Bolivia	2.5	2.7	7	40	44	3.1	+.39	5.6	6.1
Brazil	2.4	2.2	138	50	73	101	−2.71	4.0	3.01
Chile	1.8	1.7	12	72	83	9.96	−.25	2.1	2.05
Colombia	2.2	1.9	29	54	67	19.4	+.08	2.8	2.84
Costa Rica	2.6	2.4	3	38	45	1.35	+1.25	3.8	5.33
Cuba	1.5	0.9	10	58	71	7.1	+1.14	0.8	1.27
Dominican Republic	2.7	2.4	7	35	56	3.92	+.11	4.2	4.29
Ecuador	3.1	2.9	10	37	52	5.2	+2.03	3.7	5.58
El Salvador	2.7	1.2	5	39	43	2.15	−.91	4.0	2.79
Guatemala	2.8	2.9	8	34	41	3.28	+1.99	4.2	7.07
Haiti	2.0	1.8	6	18	27	1.62	+.95	4.1	6.67
Honduras	3.2	3.6	5	26	39	1.95	+2.58	5.2	9.23
Jamaica	1.5	1.5	1	38	53	0.53	−.42	3.2	2.83
Mexico	3.1	2.2	80	55	69	55	−.88	3.6	3.2
Nicaragua	3.1	3.4	3	43	56	1.68	+2.00	4.5	6.07
Panama	2.6	2.2	2	44	50	1	+1.80	2.6	4.4
Paraguay	2.8	3.2	4	36	41	1.64	+2.85	3.7	7.80
Peru	2.8	2.3	20	52	68	13.6	−.89	3.8	3.38
Uruguay	0.4	0.4	3	81	85	2.55	−2.43	0.9	0.47
Venezuela	3.5	2.9	18	72	85	15.3	−.50	3.5	3.41
United States	1.0	1.0	242	72	74	179	−2.69	2.3	1.35

Source: World Bank 1988.
[a]column 5 × column 3.
[b]$\dfrac{(\text{column 3} \times \text{column 2}) - (\text{column 6} \times \text{column 8})}{\text{column 3} - \text{column 6}}$
[c]$\dfrac{\text{column 3}}{\text{column 6}} \times \text{column 2}$.

thermore, once the rural population begins to decline in absolute terms, attention becomes increasingly focused on the urban-industrial sector for the creation of expanded opportunities. This rural population stabilization and decline does not, of course, assure such opportunities. The poverty of the city slum may be more difficult to bear than the poverty in the rural setting.

It should also be noted that part of the population classified as urban continues to work in rural areas. Some rural people working and earning their livelihood in urban areas are likewise to be expected. Nevertheless, and taking full account of these problems, it is interesting to see the substantial increase in urbanization and, in almost all cases, a stabilizing or declining growth rate of total populations in this period from the mid-1960s to the mid-1980s.

Significant changes have occurred in most Latin American economies and societies in the past three decades. These changes have occurred without any major new initiatives in land reform for the past two decades, with the exception of Nicaragua and lesser efforts in several of the other smaller nations. There have also been momentous changes in the structure of the international economy. One of the more significant of these changes has been increased dependence on global trade. This has had significant impacts on most economies, but it is especially critical for those countries having a very large foreign debt—as is the case for a number of the countries of Latin America (as well as, one should add, for the United States). Since World War II, international trade has grown at a faster rate than has global gross national product. There have been a series of other significant changes in the international economy: an integrated global capital market, a shift in the exchange rate system, increased international monetary instability, and shifts in comparative advantage (Schuh 1989, 1–10). Of this latter change, Schuh concludes as follows:

> What is clear is that comparative advantage will continue to shift on the international scene, with significant impacts on the direction and size of international trade flows. U.S. agriculture has seen Brazil take over approximately half of the international soybean market and literally dominate the international market in frozen orange juice. Developments such as this are likely to be commonplace in the decades ahead. (3)

This is no insignificant achievement on the part of Brazil. Indeed, Brazil now has the eighth-largest market economy in the world. Despite these impressive accomplishments,

> agriculture in Brazil suffers from defects traceable to its highly inegalitarian pattern of resource and income distribution. In terms of living standards for its people, Brazil does not make the list of the top fifty nations. While the theme of equity in Brazil was hotly debated by economists in the 1970s, it is doubtful whether any country in the world better illustrates the "growth with inequality" paradigm. (Thiesenhusen and Melmed-Sanjak 1990, 393).

Some critics of land reform look upon experiences such as Brazil's as evidence that the "feudal institutions of land tenure," if they ever did exist,

exist no more. Agriculture in Latin America, they say, is being rapidly transformed into a capitalist system with very respectable growth rates. Since land reform was directed at feudal institutions, this reasoning goes, there is no longer a case for land reform. We shall return to this theme later. Suffice it to say that the prospects of modernization and rapid economic growth were never totally and universally denied. The question underlying the rationale for land reform has always been, What kind of growth, for whose benefit, with what distributional consequences?

On the other hand, it is also vital to recognize that the land tenure system throughout Latin America is much more complex than the simple latifundio/minifundio dichotomy would suggest. As noted earlier, there is a great deal of diversity in this very large region, and one major aspect of this is the structural diversity within the agricultural sectors. As Thiesenhusen (1989a) points out,

> the most noteworthy change that has occurred in the land tenure system of the region in the last several decades is not redistributive land reform but the emergence of a growing (but still quite small when compared to farmland in latifundio) commercial and entrepreneurial sector made up primarily of well-managed and highly productive middle-sized and large farms. While this phenomenon was first identified as a welcome mutant to the traditional system in places like southern Brazil, much of Argentina, the central valley of Chile, northern Mexico, and parts of the Sierra in Ecuador, it is becoming more common today. (2–3)

Thiesenhusen (1989b) also notes that "while the *latifundio-minifundio* structure, *grosso modo*, is still intact, land-tenure patterns in the region are in the process of slow and evolutionary alteration" (483).

Table 5 certainly confirms that a substantial part of the food needs of Latin America are provided from small-farm production. It is estimated, moreover, that small farms produce 30 percent of agricultural exports in Costa Rica, 25.5 percent in Honduras, 40 percent in Brazil, 30 percent in Colombia, 54 percent in Mexico, 63 percent in Venezuela, and 75 percent in Bolivia (Thiesenhusen 1989c, 21–22).

There has been more dynamic evolution within the bimodal land tenure structure in Latin American countries than is ordinarily credited. Recent years have also witnessed more change in farm-size structures than were seen in the 1960s. The previously cited study of the Haneys (Haney and Haney 1989), covering the Ecuadorian province of Chimborazo, shows that the traditional hacienda and its associated forms of tenancy have virtually disappeared:

Table 5.   Latin America: Provisional Estimates of Dimensions of Entrepreneurial and
Small-Producer Agriculture at the Beginning of the 1980s (in percentages)

Indicators	Entrepreneurial Agriculture	Small Producer[a]
Number of economic units	22	78
Total area covered by the units	82	18
Cultivable area covered by the units	63	37
Area utilized by the units[b]	56	44
Domestic consumption	59	41
Export	68	32
Permanent crops	59	41
Short-cycle crops	47	53
Maize	49	51
Beans	23	77
Potatoes	39	61
Rice	68	32
Coffee	59	41
Sugarcane	79	21
Cattle	76	24
Pigs	22	78

Source: López Cordovez (1982, 26); prepared with national agricultural census data. Reproduced from Thiesenhusen (1989c, 21), Table 5.
[a]The "small producer" column covers family-type units. To differentiate between them and
the entrepreneurial units, criteria of size were used.
[b]Includes area used for crops and does not include pastureland.

Land, labor, and capital markets in the rural areas have become increasingly
vigorous and complex, as the heirs of the traditional landed gentry modernize
or abandon the countryside in favor of urban-based professions and part of the
burgeoning peasantry strives to obtain a more secure hedge in the rural areas
against the vagaries of urban subsistence. (86)

This certainly corresponds to some of the changes predicted by the de
Janvry (1981) formulation, as discussed in chapter 2.

Likewise, Forster's study (1989b) of peasant strategies in Tungurahua,
Ecuador, suggests that "the most entrepreneurial *minifundistas* in each
generation were able to capture some of the land being sold and bring it into
the peasant sphere" (25). The phenomenon of greatest interest is the source
of peasant capital for the purchase of lands. In most cases, the major portion
came from off-farm sources—either labor earnings from work off the farm
or earnings from a wide variety of entrepreneurial activities. Sometimes
these income-earning opportunities were considered more valuable than
the prospect of getting additional land.

Nonfarm Income Sources: The Informal Sector

Several recent studies examine the income sources of subsistence and semisubsistence farmers as well as those of the rural poor who migrate to urban areas. In Paraguay, the central region is most densely populated, with a heavy representation of minifundio. The government opened up new lands for colonization in provinces to the east and north of this central region. Despite the prospect of getting substantially more land, migration from the central region's minifundio to the new colonization areas was limited. The majority

> preferred to compensate the lack of sufficient agricultural land with "diagonal survival strategies." By developing a wide range of additional sources of income, most of which are not directly related to agriculture, many households have managed to obtain higher incomes than would be derived from farming, with the consequence that they have preferred not to settle in one of the colonization areas. (Zoomers 1988, 154)

These potential migrants sensed that the nonfarm income sources and opportunities near their current homes would not be available in the more remote areas of colonization. Furthermore, all the family labor would likely be needed to clear the newly obtained land. In sum, they saw that their total income would decline if they moved, even though they would have had more land at the new sites.

Participant members in some of the agrarian reform production cooperatives in Honduras have also reported substantial income from off-farm labor. More than 40 percent of a sample of 271 members reported off-farm sources of income. Almost one-fifth of off-farm earners said that these activities provided the household's major source of income, and almost half listed off-farm earnings as their second-most-important source of household income (Stringer 1989b, 377).

In fact, this appears to be a generalized phenomenon across all of Latin America. In data compiled by de Janvry and Sadoulet (1989), it appears "likely that as much as two-thirds of the farm households across Latin America derive more than half of their income from off-farm sources— principally wages from employment both in agriculture and in a wide variety of other activities, many of which are linked to agriculture through forward, backward, and final-consumption linkages" (1209–10) Furthermore, rural and urban labor markets have become more integrated. Fewer agricultural workers are recruited from among the rural landless and those on mini-sized farms, while more come from households based in rural towns or in the cities. "At the same time, the share of the rural, economically active population working in non-agricultural activities has also increased very rapidly and reached percentages such as 23 in Brazil, 16 in Ecuador, 41 in Costa Rica and 42 in Mexico" (de Janvry and Sadoulet 1989, 1210).

Similar trends are evident in Asia in several rural farming village in Bangladesh. Barua (1990) found that those who bought land between 1960 and 1984 had substantially more income from nonfarm sources than those who sold land or those who neither sold nor purchased land during this period. In fact, for those who bought land, the nonfarm sources of income were about twelve times as large as the income from farming (compared to four to five times nonfarm over farm income for the other groups). Per capita income from farming itself varied only 5–10 percent among groups.

There has been a rather spectacular revival in recent years of the concept and the important implications of the *informal sector*. Much of this can be attributed to the influential book by Hernando De Soto. The book is devoted to Peru and was published in Spanish in 1986. The English translation was published in 1989.

The informal sector seems to have provided somewhat of a safety valve for pressures that might otherwise have mounted to the point of explosion. In fact, this informal sector may indeed have decreased the pressures for land reform. These safety valves were created by the poor themselves—primarily migrants from rural areas settling in or creating the urban slums—in contrast to the safety nets created by governments to shield the less fortunate from the ill effects of technological change and inegalitarian economic growth. The significance of the informal sector was not anticipated in the 1960s or perhaps even in the 1970s. The key lesson, so it appears, is the magnificent human creativity revealed by these informal sector activities. It is a lesson that must be learned and relearned by every generation. The poor and the uneducated do not lack intelligence. Their creative undertakings under circumstances where many would give up in despair reveal a wisdom that comes only from experience.

Grassroots Development, the journal of the Interamerican Foundation, devotes most of a recent issue (vol. 13, no. 1, 1989) to a reexamination of the informal sector. Several recent books are reviewed, including two on women in the informal and household sectors (Berger and Buvinic 1988; and Chaney and Garcia Castro 1989) and one that essentially shows that the informal sector has clear limitations as well as positive features (Portes et al. 1989). This conclusion is a needed antidote to the romanticization that sometimes accompanies discussions of the informal sector or *grass-roots development* or the *underground economy* (all terms having been used to describe this phenomenon). Nevertheless, it is very important to recognize this phenomenon and to appreciate the positive elements inherent in the informal economic activities of the rural and urban poor.

In introducing the topic of the informal sector, *Grassroots Development* (1989) includes this historical note:

> The notion of the informal sector has had a checkered past. Originally formu- lated in studies of Third World urbanization commissioned by the Interna- tional Labour Office (ILO) of the U.N. during the early 1970s, the idea was adopted by others as "marginalization." Both concepts were attempts to de- scribe the ad hoc economic activities that a growing wave of unskilled and impoverished migrants—unable to find salaried jobs—were employing in or- der to scrape out a living. Cut off from the formal economy, the urban poor invented their own, using shoestring budgets to transform readily available materials into low-cost goods and services for local consumption. Untaxed, unlicensed, and unregulated by the government, the full scope of informal sector activities was unmeasured and poorly understood. (2)

The concept of an informal sector has not always been cast in a positive light. In the 1950s, and especially in the 1960s, professional recommenda- tions were more often than not to modernize economies and remove the need for informal activities. The informal sector, in this view, was a hold- over from an era of underdevelopment. Import substitution, moderniza- tion, imported technology, and industrialization were seen as key indi- cators of real development. In the 1970s, however, the Interamerican Foundation came into being, financed by direct appropriations from the U.S. Congress, specifically to work directly (rather than through govern- ments) with low-income groups and struggling cooperatives, many of which would be characterized as belonging to the informal sector. In an excellent survey of the Foundation's program impacts after one decade, Hirschman (1984) provides a refreshing analysis of what might be achieved at the grass-roots level as well as some of the bottlenecks and drawbacks. In his concluding evaluation, Hirschman describes the motiva- tion that underlies and the vision that inspires action by people who em- bark upon a new and perhaps risky course—such as collective action—to better their condition:

> They will do so precisely once they feel that better condition to be not just desirable, but to be *a thing rightfully theirs* of which they are deprived. This is the reason why the proclamation of a right has so often been, if not automati- cally self-fulfilling, at least the first step to any serious attempt to secure that right.
> The wide distance separating the actual conditions of life of countless Latin Americans from what is increasingly felt as the conditions to which they have a *right* is the source of the enormous tensions in that continent; at the same time, it is the mainspring of the manifold local efforts at overcoming that distance—efforts I have found inspiring to visit and absorbing to record. (101)

In 1974, the American States Members of the International Labour Organization reported that in the late 1960s, approximately thirty million Latin Americans fell into marginal categories. The ILO report concluded that notwithstanding high rates of expansion, the modern and intermediate economic activities comprising the formal sector of the employment market had not succeeded in generating enough new employment opportunities to keep pace with growth in the labor force. The only alternative means of survival was to create a new traditional sector (traditional in terms of income and productivity), and this was the informal sector. In Asunción, Paraguay, this sector provided 57 percent of all employment; in Santo Domingo, Dominican Republic, 50 percent (ILO 1974, 4).

Mazumdar (1975), using data compiled originally by Webb (1975), reported that the traditional sector constituted 59 percent of the total urban labor force in the combined urban areas of Peru, and 53 percent in the capital city of Lima. De Soto (1989) points out that migrants to the city, speaking also of Peru, receive a rather hostile reception. Thus if, as he says, "they want to live, trade, manufacture, transport, or even consume, the cities' new inhabitants had to do so illegally. Such illegality was not antisocial in intent, like trafficking in drugs, theft, or abduction, but was designed to achieve such essentially legal objectives as building a house, providing a service, or developing a business" (11).

Since the formal sectors could not absorb most of these new in-migrants, they had little alternative but to try to create their own opportunities. These *informals*, as De Soto refers to them, rather than surrender to anarchy, developed their own laws and institutions, which he calls the *system of extralegal norms*, to make up for the shortcomings of the official legal system; "They created an alternative order to that of the formal sector" (1989, 14). De Soto estimates that 48 percent of the economically active population and 61 percent of all work hours are devoted "to informal activities which contribute 38.9 percent of the gross domestic product (GDP)" (12).

It should be noted that while providing self-made opportunities for large numbers of people, the informal sector is hardly a panacea. While some of the employment options created via these informal sector activities are reasonably productive and provide acceptable incomes, the majority of them are likely to provide extremely low compensation. The involvement of people in some of these activities is at times more an act of sheer desperation than one of voluntary choice.

What Can Reforms Contribute Now?

There appears to be more caution and less optimism today about the prospects for land reform and its impact on the public good. Perhaps we now have a more realistic and a less romantic view. Yet realism cannot and should not lead easily to the conclusion that there is no need for land reform. The problems for which land reforms were undertaken in the past persist in many areas. Many nations have a large (and often growing) proportion of people without access to resources or opportunities. Without some public safety net, these people must bear the brunt of the negative aspects of economic growth and change (Kanel 1985b).

Any evaluation of the prospective benefits and drawbacks of land reform must also compare the consequences of alternative policies. In some criticisms of land reform, there is a hidden assumption that much more effective alternative measures are available for addressing the problems of inadequate employment, inequitable distributions, and insufficient productivity. In other words, there is an implicit notion that there are easier, less controversial, and quicker ways to benefit the rural poor. There *are* alternative measures. But one must evaluate the *relative effectiveness* of alternative ways of handling multifaceted problems. Land reform may turn out to be a halfway measure; but if alternatives are only 20 percent effective, then land reform may still be a viable option. As has been said about democracy, it's a terrible system, but it's so much better than any alternative.

Thus the question posed in the title of this chapter quite obviously cannot be answered with a simple yes or no. In the 1960s, land reform was proposed as a measure to increase productive employment, to achieve a more equitable distribution of resources and income, to enhance market demand for consumer goods and thus stimulate the industrial sector, and to maintain or increase output at lower factor costs (that is, reduced use of high social-opportunity-cost capital and increased use of low social-opportunity-cost labor). These goals are still relevant, but an additional element has been brought into the picture—the maintenance of ecological diversity and the protection of the environment.

There is today a greater professional consciousness, more widely held, of the implications of land tenure diversities and the impacts of land tenure institutions on both economic performance and environmental protection. Policies of the World Bank and the regional banks as well as the bilateral assistance agencies are more likely today to take into consideration the need to understand land tenure conditions and related rural institutions when planning infrastructural and other rural development projects. In May 1989, the Interamerican Development Bank held its second consultative meeting on the environment. Included for the first time were representatives from each member country's Non-Governmental Organizations (NGOs) having a deep interest in environmental protection (El BID 1989, 3). In the same vein,

The World Bank is "irrevocably committed" to bringing economic development and environmental protection into "creative harmony," President Bar-
ber Conable declared at a conference on "Global Environment and Human
Response Towards Sustainable Development" in Tokyo on September 11. Urg-
ing a balance between development and the environment, he said the linkage
connecting environmental degradation to poverty, unchecked population
growth, and underdevelopment must be broken (*Environmental Bulletin*
1989, 1).

Brown and Macguire (1986, 397–99) conclude that land reform is basic
for the resolution of the problems of resources and poputlation. "Fundamental to correcting the current course of agricultural stagnation, rural poverty,
deforestation, and soil loss is correction of land tenure systems. The few
countries that have tried [it] . . . need encouragement and others more
pressure" (quoted in Thiesenhusen 1989a, 40).

In a special insert, *El Diario* (15 December 1989), of Asunción, Paraguay,
carried the headline, "Tierra para los campesinos—los primeras victimas
son los bosques" (Land for the peasants—the first victims are the forests).
The story goes on to point out the massive destruction of forests in some of
the eastern provinces of the country. Large landowners fear that forested
land will be seen as land "not rationally exploited" and thus possibly subject
to expropriation. The result, it is suggested, is massive deforestation without any coherent production plan by most of these landowners.

With this new and very real concern over the ties between land tenure
institutions and environmental protection, caution is urged by Thiesenhusen lest the finger of blame be pointed at "the victim." While the environmental degradation suffered at the hands of the poor peasant may be more
visible (cultivating steep hillsides and moving into and clearing forests), the
real culprit is a rural land tenure system "which allows rich landlords to
monopolize the best resources in the region and often . . . use then waste-
fully" (Thiesenhusen 1989a, 10–11). Collins (1986) notes that "environmental deterioration cannot be understood without considering the ways in
which land tenure, credit policies, titling, and other factors condition resource management strategies of the producers who work the land" (quoted
in Thiesenhusen 1989a, 15; see also Thiesenhusen 1991).

But to return to the question of the continued necessity (or not) of land
reform it would certainly be erroneous to conclude that the issues prompting a perceived need for land reform in the 1960s have disappeared or been
resolved. Massive migration and urbanization have relieved some pressures in the countryside. Millions of rural poor have moved to the cities and
managed, through their own efforts and creativity, to eke out a living at a
level just above survival. But this can hardly be considered an adequate

strategy of development. Since little land redistribution has occurred in the past twenty years, the concentration of landholdings is not too different from what it was in 1970 (or even in 1960, in most cases). Nor is there any evidence that income is distributed more evenly.

Thiesenhusen (1989a, 11) notes that "1.3 percent of the farms occupy about half of the farm area in Colombia; the Gini coefficient for Brazil and Guatemala is in the realm of .85, and that of Paraguay, where land is probably more concentrated than in any other country in Latin America, is .94." In Brazil, Thiesenhusen estimates that there are about nine million landless in the agricultural sector. "If just the wasted land in farms were distributed in plots of 3.7 hectares, all the currently landless in Brazil [in addition to about three million who live in towns and cities but work mainly in agriculture] would be able to receive a small farm and not be forced to seek land in the Amazon or migrate to the cities" (19). Although not a long-run solution, "it would delay migration and relieve pressure on the environment for at least a generation, to allow job-offering industry to catch up with labor supply."

If the absorption of labor in Latin America's agriculture is not enhanced, future confrontations may occur in the cities as rural-to-urban migrations continue to increase. The United States did not totally escape this consequence resulting from the vary rapid transformation of its agricultural structures, especially from the 1940s through the 1960s. However, in the United States, this transformation coincided with a major expansion of the nonfarm economy and occurred at a time when the farm population had already declined very substantially from its peak numbers. Furthermore, population growth was at a much lower rate. On all these fronts, the situation in most of Latin America is very different, and the explosive potential of a growing, economically marginalized population in the urban slums must not be underestimated.

People cannot simply be "placed on hold" until they are needed by industry. They must be engaged in productive activity in order to develop the skills and discipline which both modern agriculture and industry require. An even more important impact of idleness is the depression of hopes, aspirations, and self-respect, especially among the young. Land must be viewed not merely as a factor of production to be combined efficiently with scarce capital so as to maximize agricultural output, but also as a vehicle for employing people and for developing their skills. The manner in which increased output is achieved, and the number of people who participate in and reap benefits from the experience, may be as important as the short-run production increase itself. Poverty cannot be eliminated by working only with the poor. The poor need resources that are controlled by others. "Wherever there is surplus agricultural labor and shortage of working capital, the task of the tenure system is to put people to work. This is when proposals for land distribution are most strongly compelling" (Raup 1967, 274).

It is worth noting that the greatest uncaptured opportunity within most of the developing countries is the enhancement of the human resource. Natural resources in the purely physical sense are finite; human intelligence and skills, so far as we know, are not. It is indeed a tragic waste that so many millions of people have so little opportunity to be challenged to develop their human capacities—both the powers of the mind and the skills of physical dexterity. Even the untutored and unsophisticated mind has much to contribute, given the opportunity. All individuals are potentially creative. Human skills and capacities, developed through formal schooling and work opportunities, are any nation's true and basic renewable resource. The motive force in the development process is not provided by investment plans and projects of public administrators and private entrepreneurs, important as these are. The informed self-interest and the growing skills of the mass of farmers and urban workers, and their creative human energies, are the real impulse for any long-term progress.

The human resource plays a dual role. People are resources as well as users of resources, including other people. Every individual plays this dual role—both the user and the used, the interested and the object of interest, the exploiter and the object of exploitation, the reason for development and the means of its realization (Dorner 1983, 307–8).

There is a continuous need to modify institutional rules and norms to keep this process of using others mutually beneficial. Procedures in a democratic setting are negotiated so that individuals and groups, in pursuing their private interests, are not injuring (and preferably are furthering) the interests of other individuals and groups. When mutuality in the process breaks down and conflicts intensify, the discretionary behavior of the individuals and groups involved must be redefined to reestablish mutuality in the process of associated living.

Institutions consist of rules defining for individuals their rights and privileges, their responsibilities and obligations, as well as their exposure to the protected rights and activities of others. Commons (1959) defined institutions as "collective action in restraint, liberation, and expansion of individual action" (73). "Institutional structures," says Kanel (1985a), "are devices for containing but not for resolving the tension between individuals and their private agendas on the one hand and their need for system integration and protection on the other. They are never perfect solutions and they require reevaluations and reforms; or even revolutions if they become too rigid and obsolescent" (827).

But institutional structures, imperfect as they may be in resolving these tensions, cannot be shaped by a small elite. People need to provide input regarding the design of these structures in order to "limit the arbitrariness of power" (Kanel 1985a, 825). And institutions do not stand in sectoral isolation. The consequences of a highly skewed pattern of resource ownership in the countryside permeate the urban-industrial institutional structures as well. Furthermore, such resource distribution patterns also make it more difficult to incorporate the experience of the majority into the reshaped institutional rules.

The land reforms in Taiwan and South Korea occurred early in their growth and industrialization process. The industrial sector was never as closely tied to the inegalitarian rural structures as is often the case in Latin America. When discussing the pros and cons of land reforms in Latin America, it is necessary to take a wider view, not confined to the agricultural sector. Concludes Thiesenhusen (1989b): "One can find the future bright if it is assumed that the lessons of the 1960s and 1970s are not lost on state elites and international powers who understand that positive policy must be enacted to help reconstruct the social order on a more equitable basis and forestall the social instability that will otherwise result" (484). "To help reconstruct the social order" is a broader charge than land reform.

A fundamental need is to incorporate the experience of the people into new rules and new institutional structures. This requires a greater democratization of public processes and procedures than that developed to date in most Latin American countries. De Soto (1989), in his conclusion, makes some very telling points:

> Another advantage of popular consultation is that the rule-making process would make much better use of the knowledge scattered throughout the country. In a society in which millions of people interact in billions of ways and execute thousands of contracts, in which a variety of cultures, life-styles, and viewpoints intermingle, it is inconceivable that an authority would, without consultation, have access to all the information it needs to formulate working rules or norms.
>
> A democratic system would force the government to justify, to the public, the need for a new law and to make sure that no group benefits at the expense of all. This would increase the political influence of the public in general. . . . It also means that rulers would be answerable to public opinion continuously, not just every five years. (253)

Is land reform still necessary? The land tenure conditions and the land-ownership concentrations existing in the 1960s have been modified somewhat, though not drastically. "The leading cause of rural poverty by far is the lack of access to sufficient land and low productivity of land use for a majority of the rural population" (de Janvry and Sadoulet 1989, 1209). The major changes have been in population shifts and increased industrialization. But the opportunities provided by the formal sector (either industry or agriculture) have fallen far short of the employment needs of the poor. Because the margin of food security has in some cases narrowed (given the burgeoning populations), and because agricultural exports retain a crucial role in the economy of most Latin American countries, and because the investments needed for a highly productive agriculture require stability and security of expectations, special precautions in the design and implementation of future land reforms are important. At the same time, it must be well remembered that the current system and strategy are not without substantial risks. If provision of opportunities on the land for a large segment of the currently landless were actually a top priority of government (and those with power on whom the government depends), it could be accomplished through agrarian reform policies that set clear goals and unambiguous criteria for their implementation. It could be done without catastrophic declines in investment and output due to uncertainties. Thus it can be argued that reform is still needed. But small-scale efforts with only half-hearted support, similar to many of those of the 1960s, will not suffice. Furthermore, increased attention must be given to the inclusion of some of the poorest among the rural populations, so that the benefits of land reform do not continue to go only to a small, sometimes the better-off, segment of the peasantry.

Having said all this, I believe it is also abundantly clear that land reform is not enough. Given all the structural changes that have taken place over the past thirty years, the pontential gains from even a well-structured and supported land reform are likely to be more limited than would have been the case twenty-five to thirty years ago. We must also acknowledge that land reform may hold very few economic or social benefits in some cases. Where potential economic and social benefits from a land reform are large, and where political opportunities present themselves, land reform is still needed and desirable.

Given the greater complexity of the economies in general and the employment and income sources of the rural and urban poor in particular, a package of programs in addition to land tenure adjustments and reform may be needed in most countries. De Janvry and Sadoulet (1989, 1218–20) propose such a package in their "Investment Strategies to Combat Rural Poverty: A Proposal for Latin America." Among the proposed approaches they suggest are the following:

1. "Farm-oriented rural development." These include initiatives directed toward that segment of the peasantry with sufficient resources to absorb productively most family labor on the farm.
2. "Household-oriented rural development." These are to be directed

toward the very small farms (frequently under the control of women since men often work outside the farm) for the enhancement of such activities as raising small animals and a dairy cow or two, handicrafts, trade, and transformation of agricultural products, among others.

3. "Access to land: Land reform and colonization." They also caution against the spontaneous colonization which often has led to serious ecological problems and conflicts with indigenous populations.

4. "Employment creation and labor market rationalization." Here they suggest, among other measures, the elimination of price biases and subsidies that continue to favor the diffusion of mechanical, labor-displacing innovations.

Additional suggestions are provided by two representatives of the Agricultural Operations Division of the World Bank (see Binswanger and Elgin 1990). In addition to some of the points above, they suggest the elimination of income tax exemptions for agriculture and subsidized credit for large farmers. They also call for the removal of perverse tenancy restrictions and an accelerated program to give small holders clear titles to their land.

Obviously, one could list numerous other government actions needed to help develop a progressive agriculture in which the poor would share equitably. The main purpose in listing some of these points is as a reminder that land reform alone is not enough to achieve such a goal. Several of these areas of policy action will be discussed in the next and in the final chapter.

5

Measures Related to Land Reform

Many beneficiaries of land tenure policies go unreported when the term is confined to those who actually received land via land redistribution. A number of measures enacted under the rubric of agrarian reform have beneficial consequences that are not captured by the usual counting of beneficiaries and lands affected. These measures—land registration and titling, land taxation, and land transfer and financing mechanisms—are sometimes referred to as alternatives to land reform. This is an unfortunate label. These policies are, in fact, required for an efficiently functioning agricultural economy whether or not they accompany a reform of the land-tenure system. All these policies are here considered measures related to land reform designed to create and/or improve the efficiency of the land market. It is, of course, much easier to enhance market efficiency by these measures in a relatively egalitarian landholding structure than in a highly skewed one. However, even where landownership is highly concentrated, such policies may stimulate the land market to the benefit of at least some of the poor (Dorner and Saliba 1981).

Land Registration and Titling

A land registration and titling system is an organized set of rules and legal procedures intended to govern the functioning of the registry institution in a particular country. It should pursue three main functions (Franco-García 1970):

1. Security. To protect the rights of the legal owner against interference by third persons, land registration must provide owners with indisputable evidence of title. Rights protected include the rights to use, manage, and develop the land owned and to transfer these rights by inheritance, grant, or sale (King 1979).
2. Publicity. Land registration must openly and legally inform the public about the prevailing state of landownership.

3. Transfer. Land registration must provide ways to accommodate changes in and/or limits on property rights in real estate.

By providing a clear identification of land and its owner and by stating the owner's rights as well as encumbrances, registration improves the process of transferring and marketing land. The guarantee of an owner's rights encourages productive use, and improved marketability can bring about a more efficient allocation. Increased marketability of land may also help to raise productivity by allowing consolidation of farm units and/or better access to land for small farmers or small-farmer cooperatives. If registration provides security and the information is publicly available, land titles may have many uses and applications. One of the foremost, perhaps, is providing a basis for extending credit, so that landowners are able to acquire additional resources to make their land more productive.

Legal provisions, important as they may be, are not the only needs of an efficient land registration system. Adherence to legal principles can lead to a complicated and costly titling system, but simplicity of the registration procedure is also a critical concern. Simplicity is essential if the system is to be readily understood by those who will become owners of land. Otherwise, it is unlikely that the titling program will earn the confidence of small farmers who lack legal title or of landless workers who want to acquire land. Legislative and administrative requirements should be readily intelligible and preferably translated into the vernacular language. Legalisms— including overzealous professionalism on the part of registry employees— can be counterproductive (West 1972).

Closely linked to the need for simplicity is a need for an inexpensive process of registration—a system affordable to small farmers. If the administrative steps are few and simple, the fees to be paid by owners can be reduced accordingly, as can the costs of travel to towns where registry offices are located. Another way to make titles more affordable is to fix fees for legal advice and notaries at rates linked to the value of the parcel to be titled. Such rates should of course be well publicized and uniformly applied.

Timeliness is also a critical requirement. The registration procedure, whether first inscription of title or transfer of an existing title, should be accomplishable quickly, so that owners are able to plan and invest with greater security.

Finally, a land titling system can be designed to protect those who work the land and thus encourage a more productive use of agricultural resources. A registration system should try to extend its benefits not only to holders of "superior interests"—landlords—but also to holders of "derivative interests"—tenants. Measures should be taken to improve the security of tenants and help to integrate them into a market economy. Tenancy boundaries could "be demarcated and surveyed and a memorial of each tenancy . . . entered as an encumbrance on the title of the superior interest holders" (West 1972, 3).

Stanfield (1985) has summarized the expectations about the role of secure titles:

1. A secure title enables the farmer to use the land as collateral for securing loans from financial institutions (see also Dorner and Saliba 1981).
2. A secure title provides farmers with incentives to invest in their farms by increasing the probability that the capital they accumulate will provide them with future benefits (see Raup 1967).
3. With this combination of increased *ability* to secure operational and long-term capital and the farmer's increased *incentive* to use this capital in the farm enterprise, farmers with secure title will actually increase their long-term capital investments as well as their purchase of production inputs.
4. With higher investments and greater use of production inputs, the value of production per hectare will be higher for the holdings with secure title than for those without such title. (11)

It should be noted that titling may also at times lead to the loss of land through sale by previous land reform beneficiaries to the larger and more capital-secure farmers. This is one reason why restrictions on sale are often placed for varying periods on parcels distributed under a land reform program. This, of course, in no way detracts from the desirability of land registration and titling as a general policy, though it may include such special caveats for the new land recipients. Having a secure title to the land one is operating may also provide incentives for the use of protective land conservation measures

Most Latin American countries are engaged to some degree in efforts to improve land titling and registration—but much remains to be done. Costa Rica presents an interesting case of progress in this area. From 1966 to 1985, 31,224 title deeds were granted to a total of more than half a million hectares. Most of this occurred during the last half of the 1970s and early 1980s (Grau 1990, 243). Another 12,000 titles have been issued since 1986, half of them under an AID-supported project (see Shearer et al. 1990).

Titles are also issued under land reform programs establishing collective enterprises. In such cases (for example, the state-managed farms in Nicaragua or the worker-managed farms in phase one of El Salvador's agrarian reform) individual certificates of title are typically not issued, but rather one has an implied right to work and to have noncash rights (housing, garden plot, etc.) in the collective. The individuals who desire to become members of the enterprise are evaluated and permitted to become part of a set of reform beneficiaries who work on the reform enterprises on a permanent basis. In the Salvadoran case even part-time workers are given some tenure in the sense of being assured of at least some work during the year on the cooperatives. (Schweigert 1989, 55).

As instruments of land market inetervention, land registration and titling are perhaps of secondary importance in most cases in terms of providing wider access to land for the rural poor. For this reason these programs may also arouse less political opposition. Nevertheless, many small-scale, low-income farmers are working land for which they have no clear title or land on which they subsist as tenants with insecure status. Increasing tenure security for these farmers through titling and tenancy-rights measures can and does provide substantial benefits.

Land Taxation

Land taxation policies have perhaps a greater potential for expanding access to land for the rural poor, but for this and other reasons they have also been opposed by large landowners as well as by small owners. No one wants to pay more taxes. Yet land taxation would seem to be a relatively flexible instrument: severity and gradation of the tax rate, basis and method of assessment, exemptions, special penalties, and modes of payment are all at the discretion of planners. Each of these features can be modified to build a tax designed to achieve any or all of the three frequent objectives of property taxation: (1) revenue, (2) incentives for increased productivity, and (3) incentives for redistribution of income and land. The revenue and productivity functions of property taxes may also serve to enhance the distributional function.

In agriculturally based economies, land is the most significant form of wealth and thus a major potential source of revenue. Land taxes, however, are currently an insignificant source of public funds in most developing countries. The primary and nearly universal reasons for low revenue yields from land taxation are insignificant tax rates, low assessments eroded by inflation, and lack of rigorous enforcement. These problems can be corrected. Low revenue yields in Latin America do not indicate that land taxation has little potential; rather, they illustrate the lack of a strong commitment to taxation objectives, improved tax design, and effective enforcement of tax laws.

Ideally and theoretically, land taxation can encourage redistribution of income and access to income-earning opportunities in several ways:

1. A significant tax burden encourages landowners either to use their land more productively or to sell or lease it to people who will.
2. A tax with progressively higher rates as land value and/or parcel size increase may precipitate the sale of parts of large parcels in order to escape higher tax rates.
3. Land taxation requires records on landownership and some indication of productive potential based on soil quality, topography, and access to water. These records, if made public, increase the information available to potential buyers of land.
4. Revenue from taxation can be used to finance loans to prospective buyers and to underwrite developmental infrastructure. The unpopularity of the tax may be slightly diminished if it is apparent to taxpayers that the revenues benefit them in tangible ways.
5. Special penalties can single out particularly undesirable forms of tenure (absentee ownership) for heavier tax burdens while exempting farms of more desirable size or character (family farms). However, exemptions to a general tax can easily be counterproductive. Small farmers lack information and/or legal counsel needed to take advantage of the exemption, while large owners may find ways to avoid penalties, especially if the category of property to be penalized cannot be precisely defined and identified (Dorner and Saliba 1981, 5).

But what might seem ideal in theory is not always workable in practice. According to the *World Development Report* (World Bank 1988), with a very few exceptions land taxes generate only a minor fraction of public revenue. Primary commodity export taxes are a much greater source of revenue. The low yield from land taxes reflects the inadequate land registration and land valuation procedures. Also, in many countries, rural land transactions are infrequent, which restricts the use of market prices to determine land values (World Bank 1988, 91). "With the exception of Chile and Jamaica and, to a lesser degree, Colombia, there has not been a systematic effort in any of the countries to make land taxation an effective fiscal policy tool" (Shearer et al. 1990, 39–40).

In a report (funded under a contract between USAID and Associates in Rural Development), Strasma and colleagues comment on the modifications in the Jamaican and Colombian land tax system and suggest that these have not yet had the desired effect on agricultural production or productivity. Quoting from the Sazama and Davis analysis of the Chilean experience of the 1960s, they conclude that "even if property taxes have economic effects other than raising revenue, they can easily be swamped by other changes in demand or supply conditions" (Strasma et al. 1987, 44, quoting from Sazama and Davis 1973, 650).

Land taxes can also have negative impacts, as noted in the case of Brazil:

> The Brazilian land tax has, since 1963, contained provisions for deductions ostensibly designed to encourage more intensive land use. However, in addition to undermining the progressive rates (by size), these provisions have recently been shown to have a markedly negative environmental impact. They have encouraged large-scale conversion of privately owned or claimed forest land in the Amazon to pasture or crop land where such conversion is not only ecologically destructive but would not have been economically justified without the tax provision. (Strasma et al. 1987, 49)

But land taxation could and should have positive effects. There are historical cases where such positive results were achieved—for example, in Japan and Australia in the nineteenth and early twentieth centuries (Dorner and Saliba 1981). As with redistributive reforms (and perhaps even more so), the major obstacles are at the political level. Land taxes affect all landowners, large and small, and direct benefits are very difficult to identify. Land taxation policies do not generate a political constituency. In contrast, a land redistribution has an identifiable group of potential beneficiaries who will support it.

To realize some of the positive features of a comprehensive land taxation system, governments must devise equitable and low-cost methods for assessing farmlands and for keeping these assessments current. Rate structures and levels must be high enough to produce substantial revenues and to create the other positive effects that land taxes are capable of achieving. Land taxes, as with other taxes, must be administered fairly and efficiently, and revenues should be used in ways which taxpayers consider acceptable and equitable. "While this is an ideal, experience shows that countries that come relatively closer to the ideal seem more likely to succeed in the efforts to use land tax as a development instrument" (Strasma et al. 1987, 23). Although taxation of land and improved enforcement have been widely discussd and recommended, there have been few recent changes of significance in land tax policies in the Latin American nations.

Land Transfer and Financing Mechanisms

One policy area in which there has been considerable activity, especially in Central America, is land-transfer financing mechanisms. Providing the appropriate credit instruments and institutions to serve a land market and to facilitate land transactions is a longstanding and well-recognized problem. Short-term credit for six to twelve months is usually sufficient to finance annual production costs, and three- to five-year loans may be adequate for financing machinery or livestock. But land is a perpetual resource and returns on investments in land are generally quite low. Because land is immobile and because its productive capacity is durable and renewable, banks and other lending agencies should be able to provide longer-term loans secured by mortgages on landed property. Although lenders do not as a matter of policy relish the thought of foreclosure when mortgage payments are in default, their legal right to foreclose and take the property is inherent in the mortgage contract (Dorner and Saliba 1981).

Farmland financing programs are important economic policy components in the United States and other industrialized countries. Mortgage financing has existed in several of them for over a century. The Federal Land Bank system was established in the United States in 1916. With the end of the land grants and government land sales, tenants or others who wished to purchase land and/or expand their farms needed relatively large sums of money for land purchases. Most banks, organized to serve the rapidly growing industrial sector, did not have the capacity to issue farm real-estate loans. The Federal Land Banks were created to fill this gap. In Europe, land banks date to the eighteenth century. Unlike commercial banks, which depend on savings deposits for their funds these land-bank institutions issue long-term mortgage bonds and other securities or receive their capital resources from the government. The securities are backed by the first lien on the properties purchased by the borrowers.

This broad approach to land financing has never been attempted in Latin America. Small local efforts are under way, and in the past few years, Guatemala, Honduras, St. Lucia, Brazil, and Ecuador have experimented with land-financing programs on a pilot basis. Donor agencies have also focused more attention on ways to make land markets more efficient and more accessible to the landless and land-poor among rural populations. The AID Policy Determination on Land Tenure (PD-13) (AID 1986) states that the

> A.I.D. supports those LDC policies and programs which lead to a general, country-wide reliance on market forces in the valuation and distribution of land ownership and land use rights. A.I.D. will also support programs that broaden the opportunity for access to agricultural land, promote tenure security, and stimulate productive uses of land to ameliorate the barriers to market entry that exist in some LDCs. (2)

In current Latin American economic and political contexts, the development of land-bank and land-financing programs may be a viable attempt to influence patterns of land access. There is, however, no single blueprint for a land-market strategy or land-financing program that is appropriate for all nations. Land tenure and financial structures in Latin American countries share some similar characteristics, but program and policy initiatives to make the land market more accessible to the rural poor will require attention to the particular configuration of market constraints within each country.

One such effort for helping campesinos acquire land was the Land Sale Guaranty Program financed by AID in both Ecuador and Costa Rica in the 1970s. Both were relatively small pilot projects. The purpose was to facilitate the direct sale of agricultural lands from private sellers to campesino cooperatives and to provide the buyer with agricultural credit and technical assistance. The AID loans were designed to provide a private enterprise approach to land reform. The assumption was that some landowners would be willing to sell land if they could be assured of full payment under the program's guarantees. Some land was transferred, but the programs remained small and did not spread as was hoped, largely because of lack of land offered for sale (Dorner and Saliba 1981).

Beginning in 1984, the AID mission in Guatemala funded a Commercial Land Market Project carried out by the Penny Foundation (Fundación del Centavo), a private, local development organization. Three million dollars were provided for farmland purchases, technical assistance, and production credit as well as part of the Foundation's administrative costs. Under the grant agreements, the Penny Foundation (1) negotiates the purchase of farmland on the open market, paying up to 50 percent in cash at the time of sale and the balance over a three- to five-year period through certificates of guarantee; (2) divides the farm into commercially viable, family-sized parcels; (3) selects eligible participants willing to purchase the parcels and capable of making a 10 percent down payment; (4) finances the sale of land to selected participants; and (5) provides technical assistance and production credit untill the new households become acquainted with the new crops and technology. The Penny Foundation Land Market Project is a unique effort to provide access to land for the rural poor in Guatemala (Stewart et al. 1987).

In 1987, the project was extended for another five years with an additional $7.5 million grant. The Foundation also concerns itself with other aspects of integrated rural development, including education and housing. "More than 1,700 *campesino* families, most of them previously landless, were settled on 28 farms covering 6,252 hectares in seven of Guatemala's 22 departments. Most farms grow coffee or other export crops such as vegetables" (Shearer et al. 1990, 46).

A land-purchase project in Ecuador is managed by the Fondo Ecuatoriano Popularum Progressio (FEPP). In the mid-1970s, FEPP established a rotating credit fund for land purchases. Since 1977, it has made nineteen loans to campesino groups. Loan installments are programmed to coincide with the kind of economic activity practiced on the new farm, and FEPP has thus far had no problems with late payments. It requires a minimum down payment of 10 percent, but most groups have paid more (40 percent in one instance). FEPP allows up to twelve years for repayment (some groups have repaid in less time) at interest rates that have risen from 9 percent in 1977 to 12 percent in 1982, and more recently to 16 percent, about 5 percent lower than rates on commercial loans. FEPP also requires that the group maintain responsibility for repayment by individual members.

FEPP officials have learned that assisting the buyers' group in its purchase-price negotiations is very important. In their excitement about obtaining land, the campesinos are too willing to agree to the seller's first price or too inexperienced and hesitant to counteroffer for fear of losing the land. FEPP's biggest problem is that more groups now want land than its fund allows. While FEPP averages about four farm-loan applications per month, it has been able to finance only about two sales each year (Stringer 1989a, 13–14).

Another approach to land financing, not yet implemented, has been proposed for World Bank assistance in the state of Piauí in northest Brazil. The strategy is to establish a regional land agency that buys farms on the market and redistributes them to landless and land-poor farmers. In addition to providing access to land, this project would attempt to help consolidate very small farms into commercially sized units.

In the Brazilian proposal, the land agency would coordinate financial mechanisms with local rural banks to purchase land, restructure it, and resell parcels to the landless. The Piauí Land Agency would be responsible for land acquisitions, capital improvements, redistribution, and social and economic infrastructure (such as feeder roads, water supplies, and health and education facilities). This approach is much broader than that of the other land-purchase funds described above or the established land banks of the industrialized countries. The designers of this project, recognizing that land reform on a national scale is probably politically unacceptable in Brazil, sought an alternative means of correcting the skewed land distribution (Stringer 1989a, 15).

The St. Lucian government has considered a land-financing program to address the problems of multiple ownership of family lands. About 30 percent of the agricultural land in St. Lucia has multiple owners. The program would allow one co-owner to become sole owner by buying out the others

(Stringer 1989a, 15–16). It is evident that all these programs are experimental. On an expanded scale, however, they might help to modify land markets to the benefit of the rural poor who seek land.

Although conditions are vastly different, it is worth pointing out that the Brazilian project proposed for World Bank financing has many features that are quite similar to a successful Canadian program that has been in operation for several decades. The Saskatchewan Land Bank buys land on the open market by making what it considers to be competitive bids; the seller is free to sell land to the Land Bank or to sell it on the open market. The Bank leases land to eligible young formers. Leases can continue until the farmer reaches 65 years of age, but after five years, the lessee has the option to buy the land at the prevailing market price. Upon purchase, the farmer must pay for any capital land improvements (such as clearing or drainage) financed by the Land Bank during the period of the lease. Until the time of purchase, costs of such major improvements are paid by the Land Bank, which acts as owner-landlord. When the Land Bank purchases very large farms, it may break them up and lease parcels to several individuals. The Bank does not put any great pressure on land prices in Saskatchewan because it does not outbid private buyers, but rather bids only on land that is offered to it.

The Saskatchewan program offers interesting lessons and some insights into ways by which the state can intervene in the land market. It has been able to acquire land, and dispose of it, while keeping it operating in the hands of families who have the qualifications but not the immediate finances for purchasing the land. Programs such as this also provide a means to prevent an increasing concentration of land into ever fewer hands (Dorner and Saliba 1981, 32–34).

One obstacle which often makes large landowners reluctant to sell part of their land is the complexity of subdividing their holdings and dealing with numerous small buyers. But under the several land-bank purchasing programs discussed, the seller is faced with only a single transaction with just one buyer. In this way, the land banks help to resolve the inconsistency between size of farm units offered by sellers and those wanted by buyers.

While these programs offer some promise, there are also several difficulties that need to be overcome. The first issue is the availability of sufficient funds for these projects. In the industrial countries with well-developed capital markets, land-financing institutions raise capital by issuing long-term mortgage bonds and other securities. They also have received (some still do) capital resources from the government. In developing countries, although capital markets are growing and becoming broader in scope, land-bank lending institutions still rely primarily on depositors and especially international assistance agencies for the funds to finance land-purchase transactions. Unless these land banks have very large quantities of capital, they will not be able to purchase much land and will be able to finance further purchases only when current borrowers replenish the funds through repayment. Long-term financial mechanisms must be developed for these programs if they are not simply to shut down when the grants run out (Shearer et al. 1990; Dorner and Saliba 1981; Stringer 1989a).

A second issue concerns the ability of the buyers to service their debts. "The lending institutions' assessment of the value of the farm property for which a loan is to be issued, the interest rate charged on the loan, the required down payment, as well as the length of the loan are critically important in determining the borrower's ability to repay" (Shearer et al. 1990, 44–45). Whether or not the seller of the land is paid fully for the land at the time of sale or whether part of the payment can be extended over a number of years through adequate inducements also bear upon the outcome and the potential reach of such programs.

Nevertheless, conclude Shearer et al. (1990),

Government and international development agency policies have attempted recently to affect skewed land distribution by removing obstacles to participation in the land market by land-poor and landless farmers. These interventions include land purchase and sale programs, land mortgage banks, and land registration and titling programs. (49)

This is a shift from the main thrust and policy emphasis of the 1960s.

6

Can Outside Agencies Help?
A Concluding Comment

As suggested earlier, outside agencies and international actors have relatively little influence in pushing or promoting a basic reform in another nation's institutions. "Like many politically appealing but controversial programs that need a national commitment over a long period, . . . land reform requires institutional, technological, and administrative resources that politicians, diplomants, and even international loans and grants cannot provide" (Montgomery 1984, 134–35). Even the leverage that might accompany financial assistance is not likely to entice a country's government to implement a land reform if that government is unconvinced of its advantage. The prospect of such influence was in part the philosophy underlying the Alliance for Progress, and it proved disappointing in terms of prompting governments to carry out an actual land reform rather than simply passing some legislation. It is much more productive to be supportive of reform once the political decision has been taken internally and provided it is judged to be a sincere and promising effort. "Intervention at the highest levels of policy," concludes Montgomery, "should occur only when political access or receptivity is great" (228–29).[1]

To the extent that poverty and land-related grievances breed insurgency, which threatens both national and international security, land reform can be an effective antidote. As Thiesenhusen (1985) suggests,

> in one sense, land reform can be thought of as patronage from government—
> the price of political support. This appears often to apply within countries and
> internationally. When a government acts to secure peasants on the land who
> might ordinarily be swept up by insurgents, it ensures peasant support. When
> a foreign government helps with land reform, it is part of counterinsurgency, of
> "winning their hearts and minds." Most of the time, this will result in a large
> number of beneficiaries: the government, the peasant, the economy, and the
> foreign power that protects the government. The losers are the insurgents and
> the landlords. (798)

1. See Montgomery (1984) for an excellent discussion of all these points, especially his chapter 6, "United States Advocacy of International Land Reform," and his chapter 9, "Prospects of International Action."

The question remains, at least for Latin America, whether future U.S. policy will come "to be as favorably inclined to homegrown reforms as to ones that are sanctioned and controlled by the U.S. government from the outset" (Thiesenhusen 1989b, 494). The reforms in Japan, Taiwan, and South Korea are key examples of the latter variety. But the United States held a totally different position in supporting these reforms than it has had or is likely to have anywhere in Latin America. It will not be fruitful for the United States to assume that these positive and relatively successful agrarian reforms can be duplicated in areas under quite different geopolitical circumstances.

We must expect the process of reform to be rather disorderly, almost by definition. The intellectual explication of the process cannot come from a single discipline. And the policy guidelines cannot be formulated by outsiders. Land reform involves changes, adjustments, and adaptations of a whole matrix of institutions, not only those of land tenure. The meshing and interconnecting of an institutional system are not easily grasped by people who are foreign to the society and the culture. Caution, patience, and a willingness to learn must characterize and accompany our assistance. As Patch (1965) has suggested, we must strive to emerge "with ideas of what is possible and what is impossible within the whole web of . . . culture and behavior" (5).

In all cases where outside agencies have an interest in helping countries to carry out land reforms, improved and up-to-date knowledge will be critical. Research into experiences with land reform in countries where it has been and is being carried out is essential. There is also a need for *field research* into the tremendous diversities of land tenure institutions and systems. Overgeneralization can be dangerous and should be avoided. Action based on a misunderstanding of the existing tenure conditions and institutions can lead to disastrous results. Effective implementation of complex policy decisions involving land reform requires that the diversity of tenure forms and their consequences be fully understood. Tenure forms known by the same name may vary widely in their specific arrangements not only from one country to another but also in many cases in different areas within a single nation.

In the difficult efforts at institutional reform and the attempt by outside agencies to be helpful in the process, it does appear that certain international actors or agencies have particular competencies and comparative advantages. A multilateral funding source such as the World Bank may have more restrictions with respect to certain forms of assistance than a bilateral assistance agency. A bilateral agency representing a smaller, more neutral national power such as Sweden may have major advantages in certain sensitive areas where one of the major powers would not. The motives and interests of both the United States and the Soviet Union (among others) have frequently been called into question. Such differences in comparative advantage need to be better understood; this understanding could be aided by research that would help to improve future responses by different international actors. In all cases, a mode of assistance has to be compatible with a developing country's genuine fears of geopolitics and economic imperialism, on the one hand, and its urgent need for growth with equity on the other.

In most cases, probably the least controversial (and sometimes the most helpful) form of assistance is the provision of analytical skills via well-trained technical advisors and the support of scholars, students, and government workers for specialized training. Yet technical assistance is neither always nor necessarily keyed to the special needs and problems faced by specific countries. In a rather sweeping indictment, Dovring (1988) suggests that a

> very special case of American misconception about conditions in low-income countries involves land reform. American advisors in the 1950s and 1960s were against it, in India, Vietnam, Latin America, and elsewhere, in situations where such reforms should have had a high order of priority if those countries were to embark on the kind of societal development that Americans like most. The 'land reform ex ante' in the free-settler countries is one basic fact that has receded so far into the past that it is overlooked nowadays. (300)

The need for financial assistance from outside agencies for implementing land reforms can be broken down into several categories: (1) land acquisition and transfer costs, (2) administrative costs, and (3) consolidation costs and the funding of supporting services (infrastructure, marketing, credit, titling, and so forth) (Lin, Sein 1990, 29).

Neither multilateral nor bilateral assistance agencies have particular political or other difficulties with categories 2 or 3, always assuming that the proposed projects and programs are well designed and hold promise for meeting the objectives sought. In fact, requests for financing in those categories may not be related to land reform. General rural development projects would have some of the same needs with or without the land redistribution that is the centerpiece of land reform.

It is financing for category 1 that creates problems for most external donors. What rationale could be used to justify external financing for paying landlords for the land expropriated from them? This would seem to be an internal matter to be resolved solely by the private and public actors and powers indigenous to a nation. In many cases, international assistance is difficult to justify to voters even for such widely supported causes as the strengthening of special programs to reduce hunger and the worst kinds of degrading poverty. There are suspicions that the money will go to those not really in need and that the poor will see little benefit. Justifying the use of tax monies to pay for land expropriated from landlords half a world away would be nearly impossible. These are arguments frequently heard, and it would be very difficult for any politician to support the use of international assistance (loans or grants) for this purpose. While flexibility of foreign assistance is critical for the effective support of land reform, helping to buy out the landlords may be pressing the need for flexibility too far. AID's Policy Determination Paper (1986) on land tenure makes no mention of using AID funds for such purposes. Furthermore, there are congressional prohibitions against such use unless the president determines that such assistance will specifically further the interests of the United States (Sec. 1208 of the International Security and Development Cooperation Act of 1985, Public Law 99-83, 99 Stat. 277).

There have been several proposals to create an international fund to guarantee payment to landlords for expropriated land (Montgomery 1984). One was proposed by Prosterman (1972):

> American aid in this area should be used chiefly to support a guarantee, preferably through a multilateral agency, that the bonds issued to the landlords will be paid. Either by a direct guarantee of the bonds, or a guarantee of the adequacy of the sinking fund used to retire them, landlords can be given a 'Federal Deposit Insurance Corporation' type of assurance that the bonds are safe. (139)

Adelman made a more elaborate proposal (1980):

> I would like to see the establishment of a Land Reform Fund. This Fund would be either a new international institution or a new facility within an existing international institution. It would be established expressly to design, promote, and support integrated rural development processes, including, but not limited to, the necessary land and tenurial reforms. A major initial task of the Fund would be to underwrite—that is, to insure—the compensation for expropriated land undertaken at the national level (there are international precedents for this sort of guarantee in the urban industrial sector in the activities of the Import-Export Bank). In addition, a great deal of technical and financial assistance would need to be forthcoming from the Land Reform Fund in support of the design and implementation of both the land reform itself and the rural development programs which are essential for success. The Fund would, therfore, need both international capitalization and a reasonably large technical staff consisting of specialists in agrarian reform and in rural development. (446–47)

These proposals have gained little support from international donors. Questions have been raised about such international-fund guarantees on at least two grounds. There is always an element of subsidy in "soft loans." To the extent that they would be used for compensation (and this use could be very substantial), the loans would in effect redistribute wealth in favor of the already better-off landlords. The other concern is that the guarantors could have no control over the risk assumed without direct interference with national sovereignty in determining the amount and form of compensation and the whole array of repayment provisions by the land reform's beneficiaries (see Lin, Sein 1990, 40).

It should also be noted that an idea similar to that of a guarantee fund was, in effect, tried on a very small scale (see chapter 5) in the Land Sale Guaranty Programs financed by AID funds in Ecuador and Costa Rica in the 1970s. These programs were specifically designed to provide a guarantee to the seller that the finances to pay for the land were assured. As noted, the programs remained small and landowners did not rush forward offering to sell their land. It should also be noted, however, that the key difference here was that these funds were not to pay landowners for *expropriated* lands. Selected landowners were sought who would be willing to sell their land with the guarantee of full payment.

Although the use of AID funds for compensating expropriated landlords for their land is not likely, the United States has invested very substantial assistance funds in land reforms and related programs. Drawing upon figures supplied by the Agency for International Development, Montgomery (1984, 3) concludes as follows:

> American support for land reform, land settlement, land development, and land management and conservation totaled $3.9 billion in AID obligations from 1978 to 1983. Direct assistance to land reform as such amounted to $2.8 billion; settlement, $104 million; development, $71 million; and management and conservation, $197 million. . . . Additional U.S. support included extension, $281 million; water development, $289 million; credit, $206 million; inputs, $483 million; marketing, $58 million; and institutional development, $106 million.

Whether or not and at what level such assistance by the United States, by other industrial bilateral donor nations, and by the international multilateral sources will continue is uncertain. But while the land-sale guarantee programs of the 1970s did not offer appropriate inducements for landowners to offer sufficient land for sale, these conditions, too, are changing. Some of the land-bank puchase-resale programs of the 1980s were restricted primarily by lack of funds and not by lack of available land for purchase. With increasing growth in business and industrial sectors, and with expanding national capital markets, land is losing some of its appeal as an investment asset.

International donors can help nations provide greater opportunities for the rural poor through intervention and improvements in land markets. What may indeed become an increasingly productive form of such intervention is the provision of specialized mortgage credit via an intermediary land bank or similar institution which can purchase large units of land for resale to individuals and groups currently lacking the wherewithal to enter into such transactions on their own.

This approach, it should be noted, is quite different from an international fund to guarantee payment for expropriated land. External donors could provide loans for establishing such a "land bank" and thereby create a market mechanism for giving access to land to those without the necessary financial resources (but with all other qualifications for being productive farmers). This could be a loan fund to be amortized over a long period of time. As for the fund itself, land rental and/or amortization payments should make it self-renewing after a certain volume of land has been acquired.

One should not expect all land problems to be resolved by such efforts. A strong emphasis on land-market programs, however (with continuing support for such programs as settlement and colonization, where that is possible; land development and conservation; land registration and titling; credit; inputs; marketing; and so forth), could be very supportive of a movement toward growth with equity in the rural sectors.

Finally, *and not to be forgotten*, is the prospect for channeling assistance to the informal sector. This type of assistance can perhaps best be provided by NGOs (nongovernmental organizations) or special foreign assistance agencies such as the Inter-American Foundation. Such groups can and do work directly with people and groups at the local level rather than through governments. Even small amounts of resources made available to meet critical needs at strategic times can make a great deal of difference. This is quite evident when we note what people have indeed accomplished on their own without any (or very little) assistance from the outside. These efforts and accomplishments are what Hirschman (1984) found so "inspiring to visit and absorbing to record" (see chapter 4).

Final Comments

In some countries of Latin America, basic redistributive land reforms could still make a major difference in the prospect of achieving growth with improved equity. But if past experience offers any guide, achievements will be spotty unless the political commitment is sufficient to press these reforms to completion. Where such commitment is judged to exist, the United States and other internaitonal donors should lend positive support to such efforts. Meanwhile and elsewhere, there is likely to be a major role for various land-market interventions that may provide increased access to land and productive opportunities for at least some of the rural poor, and yield some prospect for evolutionary change in such markets in the future.

The very processes of growth and the introduction of new technologies call for institutional innovations and modifications whether or not land reform per se is possible. Industrial development requires the establishment of a new institutional order consistent with this expanding sector, but agricultural development must deal with an old, preexisting institutional legacy. These preexisting institutions must, over time, be modified and restructured in many ways because they were designed to serve objectives quite different from those of equitable economic growth and development.

Except for the new countries, which never labored under traditional agrarianism (but recall the U.S. Civil War, as noted in chapter 1), this transformation process has frequently been violent and disorderly. Historical analysis provides few clues as to whether a particular nation is today approaching such an upheaval or whether its rate of progress in transforming its institutions is sufficient to meet the demands and the needs of all its citizens. In fact, the revolutions associated with this transformation have sometimes occurred very early in the process of industrialization, whereas at other times they were long delayed (Dorner 1971, 14–15).

As we approach the twenty-first century, it is only too evident that conditions are quite different from those of the eighteenth, the nineteenth, or even most of the twentieth century. On a superficial level at least, it appears that the powers of the state are more formidable, making it easier to repress the interests of the masses. Yet the people of Nicaragua did turn out its dictator in 1979, and ten years later, the people of Paraguay deposed its dictator of thirty-four years. The rapidity of events in Eastern Europe during the latter half of 1989, demonstrating the strong and clearly expressed will of the people, should give pause to those who might believe that the popular will can forever be denied its expression. On the other hand, there is the irresistible pull of industrialization and urbanization. Will future explosions be led by the urban poor? Or will the urban poor by their own creative efforts be able to create an economy within an economy via the informal sector? These are serious questions that are without answers. We do know that a modern economy and society in today's complex and increasingly interdependent world will not operate very well unless most of the people pull together most of the time.

References

Index

References

Adelman, Irma. 1980. "Income Distribution, Economic Development, and Land Reform." *American Behavioral Scientist* 23 (January/February): 437–56.

Adelman, Irma, and Cynthia Morris. 1973. *Economic Growth and Social Equity in Developing Countries.* Stanford, Calif.: Stanford University Press.

Ahluwalia, Montek S. 1976. "Inequality, Poverty and Development." *Journal of Development Economics* 3 (December): 307–42.

AID (Agency for International Development). 1986. "Land Tenure." Policy Determination Paper, no. 13. Washington, D.C.: AID. 9 May.

AID (Agency for International Development). 1989. "Report from the Agency for International Development Team Assessing the Potential for Limited A.I.D. Technical Assistance to the Government of Paraguay for Agrarian Reform." Washington.

Apthorpe, Raymond. 1979. "The Burden of Land Reform in Taiwan: An Asian Model Land Reform Re-Analysed." *World Development* 7: 519–30.

Bardhan, Pranab K. 1973. "Size Productivity and Returns to Scale: An Analysis of Farm Level Data in Indian Agriculture." *Journal of Political Economy* 81: 1370–86.

Barraclough, Solon. 1984. Review of *Agrarian Crisis and Reformism in Latin America,* by Alain de Janvry. *Economic Development and Cultural Change* 32(3): 639–49.

Barraclough, Solon, ed. 1973. *Agrarian Structure in Latin America.* In collaboration with Juan Carlos Collarte. Lexington, Mass.: Heath.

Barraclough, Solon, and Authur L. Domike. 1966. "Agrarian Structure in Seven Latin American Countries." *Land Economics* 42: 391–424.

Barua, Teen. 1990. "Impact of Farm and Non-Farm Activities on Rural Income Distribution and Agricultural Development: A Study of a Village in Bangladesh." Ph.D diss., Urban and Regional Planning, University of Wisconsin–Madison.

Basu, K. 1984. "Implicit Interest Rates, Usury and Isolation in Backward Agriculture." *Cambridge Journal of Economics* 8: 145–59.

Berger, Marguerite, and Mayra Buvinic, eds. 1988. *La Mujer en el Sector Informal: Trabajo Femenino y Microempresa en América Latina.* Caracas: Editorial Nueva Sociedad.

Berry, R. Albert, and Willian R. Cline, eds. 1979. *Agrarian Structure and Productivity in Developing Countries.* Baltimore: Johns Hopkins University Press.

Bhalla, S. 1979. "Farm Size, Productivity and Technical Change in Indian Agriculture." Appendix A in Berry and Cline 1979, 141–93.

Binswanger, Hans P. 1987. "Fiscal and Legal Incentives with Environmental Effects on the Brazilian Amazon." World Bank Discussion Papers, no. ARU69. Washington, D.C.: World Bank. May.

Binswanger, Hans P., and Miranda Elgin. 1990. "What Are the Prospects for Land Reform?" In *Agriculture and Governments in an Interdependent World: Proceedings of the Twentieth International Conference of Agricultural Economists, August 1988.* Brookfield, Vt.: Gower, 739–54.

Boer, Leen, Dieke Buijs, and Benno Galjart, eds. 1985. *Poverty and Interventions: Cases from Developing Countries.* Leiden: Institute of Cultural and Social Studies, University of Leiden, 111–31.

Bromley, Daniel. 1984. Comments on "The Role of Land Reform in Economic Development: Policies and Politics," by Alain de Janvry. In *Agricultural Development in the Third World,* ed. Carl E. Eicher and John M. Staatz. Baltimore: Johns Hopkins University Press, 275–77.

Brown, Janet Welsh, and Andrew Macguire. 1986. "Saying Aye or Nay." In *Bordering on Trouble: Resources and Politics in Latin America,* ed. Andrew Macguire and Janet Welsh Brown. Bethesda, Md.: Adler and Adler, 397–99.

Brown, Marion. 1971. "Peasant Organizations as Vehicles of Reform." In Dorner 1971b, 189–206.

Brown, Marion. 1979. "Agrarian Reform and Rural Development in Developing Countries: an Overview." In *Background Papers for the United States Delegation,* World Conference on Agrarian Reform and Rural Development FAO Rome 1979. Washington: Agency for International Development, Working Group on WCARRD. July, 6–34.

Brown Marion. 1989. "Radical Reformism in Chile: 1964–1973." In Thiesenhusen 1989d, 216–39.

Bruce, John, Randy Stringer, and J. David Stanfield. 1989. "Reform among the Smallholders: St. Lucia, Jamaica, and Implications for the Caribbean." In Thiesenhusen 1989d, 338–57.

Cámara, Dom Helder. 1969. *The Church and Colonialism.* Denville, N.J.: Dimension Books.

Cámara, Dom Helder. 1979. *The Conversions of a Bishop.* An interview with José de Broucker. London: Collins.

Cardoso, F. H. 1972. "Dependency and Underdevelopment in Latin America." *New Left Review* no. 74: 83–95.

Carter, Michael R. 1984. "Identification of the Inverse Relationship between Farm Size and Productivity: An Empirical Analysis of Peasant Agicultural Production." *Oxford Economic Papers* 36: 131–45

Carter, Michael R. 1988. "Equilibrium Credit Rationing of Small Farm Agriculture." *Journal of Development Economics* 28, no. 1 (March): 83–103.

Carter, Michael R., and Elena Alvarez. 1989. "Changing Paths: The Decollectivization of Agrarian Reform Agriculture in Coastal Peru." In Thiesenhusen 1989d, 156–87.

Carter, Michael R., and Jon Jonakin. 1987. "The Economic Case for Land Reform: An Assessment of the 'Farm Size/Productivity' Relation and Its Impact on Policy." Madison: Department of Agricultural Economics, University of Wisconsin.

Carter, Michael R., and Don Kanel. 1985. "Tenancy Reform and Economic Development." Madison: Department of Agricultural Economics, University of Wisconsin. August.

Carter, Michael R., and Dina Mesbah. 1990. "Land Reform and the Rural Poor in Latin America: The Future of State-Mandated and Market-Mediated Shifts in the Structure of Land Ownership." Unpublished MS. Madison, WI.

Chaney, Elsa M., and Mary García Castro. 1989. *Muchachas No More: Household Workers in Latin America and the Caribbean.* Philadelphia: Temple University Press.

Chonchol, Jacques. 1989. "El desarrollo y la reforma agraria en América Latina." *Boletín de Estudios Latinamericanos y del Caribe* 46 (June): 3–15.

Clark, Ronald J. 1971. "Agrarian Reform: Bolivia." In Dorner 1971b, 129–64.

Collins, Jane L. 1986. "Smallholder Settlement of Tropical South America: The Social Causes of Ecological Destruction." *Human Organization* 45: 1–10.

Commons, John R. 1957. *Legal Foundations of Capitalism.* Reprint. Madison: University of Wisconsin Press. Originally published in 1924 by the Macmillan Company.

Commons, John R. 1959. *Institutional Economics: Its Place in Political Economy.* Vol. 1. Madison: University of Wisconsin Press. Originally published in 1934 by the Macmillan Company.

Congressional Record. 1965. Proceedings and Debates of the 89th Congress, First Session, vol. 3, part 18, September 14–23, 1965. Washington: U.S. Government Printing Office.

Conrad, Alfred H., and John R. Meyer. 1964. *The Economics of Slavery.* Chicago: Aldine.

de Janvry, Alain. 1981. *The Agrarian Question and Reformism in Latin America.* Baltimore: Johns Hopkins University Press.

de Janvry, Alain, and Elisabeth Sadoulet. 1989. "Investment Strategies to Combat Rural Poverty: A Proposal for Latin America." *World Development* 17: 1203–21.

Deolalikar, A. 1981. "The Inverse Relationship between Productivity and Farm Size: A Test Using Regional Data from India." *American Journal of Agricultural Economics* 63: 275–79.

De Soto, Hernando. 1989. *The Other Path: The Invisible Revolution in the Third World.* New York: Harper and Row.

Diskin, Martin. 1989. "El Salvador: Reform Prevents Change." In Thiesenhusen 1989d, 429–50.

Dorner, Peter. 1971a. "Land Tenure Institutions." In *Institutions in Agricultural Development,* ed. Melvin G. Blase. Ames: Iowa State University Press, 14–31.

Dorner, Peter. 1972. *Land Reform and Economic Development.* Harmondsworth, England: Penguin Books.

Dorner, Peter. 1979. "Rural Development Problems and Policies: The United States' Experience." In *Background Papers for the United States Delegation,*

World Conference on Agrarian Reform and Rural Development FAO Rome 1979. Washington: Agency for International Development, Working Group on WCARRD. July, 35–104.

Dorner, Peter. 1983. "Developmental Dilemmas and Paradoxes: A Personal Philosophical Note." In *Population Growth and Urbanization in Latin America*, ed. John M. Hunter, Robert N. Thomas, and Scott Whitford. Cambridge, Mass.: Schenkman, 293–310.

Dorner, Peter. 1986. "Who Should Own the Earth?" Review of *Land Reform American Style*, ed. Charles C. Geisler and Frank J. Popper, 1984. *Growth and Change* 17: 76–77.

Dorner, Peter, ed. 1971b. *Land Reform in Latin America: Issues and Cases.* Land Economics Monograph Series, no. 3. Madison: Published by *Land Economics* for the Land Tenure Center at the University of Wisconsin.

Dorner, Peter, and Don Kanel. 1971. "The Economic Case for Land Reform: Employment, Income Distribution, and Productivity." In Dorner 1971b, 41–56.

Dorner, Peter, and Don Kanel. 1977. "Introduction: Some Economic and Administrative Issues in Group Farming." In *Cooperative and Commune: Group Farming in the Economic Development of Agriculture*, ed. Peter Dorner. Madison: University of Wisconsin Press, 3–11.

Dorner, Peter, and Bonnie Saliba. 1981. "Interventions in Land Markets to Benefit the Rural Poor." LTC Research Paper, no. 74. Madison: Land Tenure Center, University of Wisconsin.

Dorner, Peter, and William C. Thiesenhusen. 1990. "Selected Land Reforms in East and Southeast Asia: Their Origins and Impacts." *Asian-Pacific Economic Literature* 4: 65–95.

Dos Santos, T. 1970. "The Structure of Dependency." *American Economic Review* 60: 231–36.

Dos Santos, T. 1973. "The Crisis of Development Theory and the Problem of Dependence in Latin America." In *Underdevelopment and Development*, ed. H. Bernstein. Harmondsworth: Penguin, 57–80.

Dovring, Folke. 1969. "Land Reform and Productivity: The Mexican Case, Analysis of Census Data." LTC Paper, no. 63. Madison: Land Tenure Center, University of Wisconsin.

Dovring, Folke. 1988. *Progress for Food or Food for Progress?* New York: Praeger.

Drake, Louis S. 1952. "Comparative Productivity of Share and Cash-Rent Systems of Tenure." *Journal of Farm Economics* 34: 535–50.

Dussel, Enrique. 1976. *History and the Theology of Liberation.* Maryknoll, N.Y.: Orbis Books.

Edwards, Everett E. 1940. "The First 300 Years." In *Farmers in a Changing World: The Yearbook of Agriculture, 1940.* Washington: U.S. Government Printing Office, 171–276.

El BID (Banco Interamericano de Desarrollo), June 1989, 1–16.

El Diario (Asunción, Paraguay), 15 December 1989.

Environmental Bulletin (World Bank), August/September 1989.

Feder, Gershon. 1985. "Relation between Farm Size and Farm Productivity: The Role of Family Labor Supervision and Credit Constraints." *Journal of Development Economics* 18: 297–313.

Feder, Gershon, Tongroj Onchan, Yangyuth Chalamwong, and Chira Hongladarom. 1986. "Land Ownership Security, Farm Productivity, and Land Policies in Rural Thailand." Prepared for World Bank Project, no. RPO-673-33. Washington: World Bank.

Fei, J. C. H., G. Ranis, and S. W. Y. Kuo. 1978. "Growth and Family Distribution of Income by Factor Components." *Quarterly Journal of Economics* 92 (February): 17–53.

Felstehausen, Herman. 1971. "Agrarian Reform: Colombia." In Dorner 1971b, 167–83.

Forster, Nancy R. 1989a. "*Minifundistas* in Tungurahua, Ecuador: Survival on the Agricultural Ladder." In Thiesenhusen 1989d, 92–126.

Forster, Nancy R. 1989b. "When the State Sidesteps Land Reform: Alternative Peasant Strategies in Tungurahua, Ecuador." LTC Paper, no. 133. Madison: Land Tenure Center, University of Wisconsin. April.

Franco-García, José María. 1970. "The Legal Insecurity of Landed Property in Venezuela: A Case Study of the Registry and Cadastral Systems." Ph.D. diss., Law and Agricultural Economics, University of Wisconsin.

Frank, A. G. 1967. *Capitalism and Underdevelopment in Latin America*. New York: Monthly Review Press.

Frank, A. G. 1969. *Latin America: Underdevelopment or Revolution*. New York: Monthly Review Press.

Furtado, C. 1963. *Economic Growth of Brazil*. Berkeley: University of California Press. Originally in Portuguese. 1959.

Furtado, C. 1965. *Diagnosis of the Brazilian Crisis*. Berkeley: University of California Press. Originally in Portuguese. 1964.

Furtado, C. 1966. "U.S. Hegemony and the Future of Latin America." *World Today* 22(9): 375–82.

Furtado, C. 1970. *Economic Development of Latin America; A Survey from Colonial Times to the Cuban Revolution*. Cambridge: Cambridge University Press. Available in Portuguese. 1969.

Galbraith, John K. 1951. "Conditions for Economic Change in Underdeveloped Countries." *Journal of Farm Economics* 33: 689–96.

Geisler, Charles C., and Frank J. Popper, eds. 1984. *Land Reform American Style*. Totowa, N.J.: Rowman and Allanhold.

Ghose, A. K. 1979. "Farm Size and Land Productivity in Indian Agriculture: A Reappraisal." *Journal of Development Studies* 16 (October): 27–49.

Gothlieb, Martin. 1987. "But Vigilance Can Become Self-Defeating." *International Herald Tribune*, 23 January.

Goulet, Denis. 1974. *A New Moral Order, Studies in Development Ethics and Liberation Theology*. Maryknoll, N.Y.: Orbis Books.

Grassroots Development (Interamerican Development Foundation), vol. 13, no. 1, 1989.

Grau, Oscar Emilio Zeledón. 1990. "The Agrarian Development Institute in the Evolution of the Pressure on Land, and its Contribution to the Development of the Costa Rican Peasant." In *Land Reform in Central America and the Caribbean*. Guatemala: Centro Impresor Piedra Santa, 215–46.

Griffin, Keith B., and A. K. Ghose. 1979. "Growth and Impoverishment in the Rural Areas of Asia." *World Development* 7: 361–83.

Haney, Emil B., Jr., and Wava G. Haney. 1989. "The Agrarian Transition in Highland Ecuador: From Precapitalism to Agrarian Capitalism in Chimborazo." In Thiesenhusen 1989d, 70–91.

Hayami, Yujiro, and Masao Kikuchi. 1981. *Asian Village Economy at the Crossroads: An Economic Approach to Institutional Change*. Tokyo: University of Tokyo Press.

Hayami, Yujiro, and Vernon W. Ruttan. 1971. *Agricultural Development: An International Perspective*. Baltimore: Johns Hopkins University Press.

Hayami, Yujiro, and Vernon W. Ruttan. 1985. *Agricultural Development: An International Perspective*. Rev. and Exp. Ed. Baltimore: Johns Hopkins University Press.

Hirschman, Albert O. 1961. *Latin American Issues*. New York: Twentieth Century Fund.

Hirschman, Albert O. 1963. *Journeys Toward Progress*. New York: Twentieth Century Fund.

Hirschman, Albert O. 1968. "The Political Economy of Import-Substituting Industrialization in Latin America." *Quarterly Journal of Economics* 82 (February): 1–32.

Hirschman, Albert O. 1984. *Getting Ahead Collectively*. New York: Pergamon Press.

Huntington, Samuel P. 1968. *Political Order in Changing Society*. New Haven, Conn.: Yale University Press.

ILO (International Labor Organization). 1974. "Improvement of the Conditions of Life and Work of Peasants, Agricultural Workers and Other Comparable Groups." Report of the Tenth Conference of American States Members of the International Labor Organization, Mexico City. November–December.

Inter-American Economic and Social Council. 1961. "Charter of Punta del Este, Establishing an Alliance for Progress within the Framework of Operation Pan America." In *Alliance for Progress: Official Documents Emanating from the Special Meeting of the Inter-American Economic and Social Council at the Ministerial Level, held in Punta Del Este, Uruguay, from August 5 to 17, 1961*. Washington: Pan American Union.

Jarvis, Lovell S. 1989. "The Unraveling of Chile's Agrarian Reform, 1973–1986." In Thiesenhusen 1989d, 240–75.

Johnston, Bruce F., and John W. Mellor. 1961. "The Role of Agriculture in Economic Development." *American Economic Review* 51: 566–93.

Kaimowitz, David. 1989. "The Role of Decentralization in the Recent Nicaraguan Agrarian Reform." In Thiesenhusen 1989d, 384–407.

Kanel, Don. 1985a. "Institutional Economics: Perspectives on Economy and Society." *Journal of Economic Issues* 19: 815–28.

Kanel, Don. 1985b. "Land Tenure and Development: The Need for Safety

Nets." Contributed paper to 19th International Conference of Agricultural Economists, held in Málaga, Spain, 26 August–4 September.

Kikuchi, Masao, and Yujiro Hayami. 1978. "Agricultural Growth Against a Land Resource Constraint: A Comparative History of Japan, Taiwan, Korea, and the Philippines." *Journal of Economic History* 38: 839–64.

King, David J. 1979. "Research Issues of Land Mapping, Titling and Registration in Indonesia, Philippines and Thailand." Preliminary. Madison: Land Tenure Center, University of Wisconsin.

Kuznets, Simon. 1955. "Economic Growth and Income Inequality." *American Economic Review* 45 (March): 1–28.

Kuznets, Simon. 1966. *Modern Economic Growth: Rate, Structure and Spread.* New Haven, Conn.: Yale University Press.

Lastarria-Cornhiel, Susana. 1989. "Agrarian Reforms of the 1960s and 1970s in Peru." In Thiesenhusen 1989d, 127–55.

Lehmann, David. 1978. "The Death of Land Reform: A Polemic." *World Development* 6: 339–45.

Lehmann, David. 1986. "Sharecropping and the Capitalist Transition in Agriculture: Some Evidence from the Highlands of Ecuador." *Journal of Development Economics* 23: 333–54.

Lin, Sein. 1990. "Financing of Land Reform in Latin America and Asia." In *Land Reform in Central America and the Caribbean.* Guatemala: Centro Impresor Piedra Santa, 27–57.

Lin, Shih-Tung. 1990. "Multiple Services Undertaken by Farmers' Associations as Measures Supportive of Land Reform in Taiwan." In *Land Reform in Central America and the Caribbean.* Guatemala: Centro Impresor Piedra Santa, 157–83.

Long, Erven J. 1961. "The Economic Basis of Land Reform in Underdeveloped Economies." *Land Economics* 37 (May): 113–23.

López Cordovez, Luis. 1982. "Trends and Recent Changes in the Latin American Food and Agriculture Situation." *CEPAL Review*, no. 16 (April).

Marini, R. M. 1965. "Brazilian 'Interdependence' and Imperialist Integration." *Monthy Review* 17(7): 10–29.

Marini, R. M. 1972. "Brazilian Sub-Imperialism." *Monthly Review* 23 (February): 14–24.

Máspero, Emilio. 1964. "Latin America's Labor Movement of Christian Democratic Orientation as an Instrument of Social Change." In *Religion, Revolution, and Reform*, ed. William V. D'Antonio and Fredrick B. Pike. New York: Praeger, 161–81.

Mazumdar, Dipak. 1975. "The Urban Informal Sector." Bank Staff Working Paper, no. 211. Washington, D.C.: International Bank for Reconstruction and Development. July.

Meier, Gerald. 1964. *Leading Issues in Development Economics.* New York: Oxford University Press.

Melmed, Jolyne S. 1988. "Interpreting the Parcellation of Peruvian Agricultural Producer Cooperatives." LTC Paper, no. 96. Madison: Land Tenure Center, University of Wisconsin.

Meyer, Carrie A. 1989. *Land Reform in Latin America: The Dominican Case.* New York: Praeger.

Montgomery, John D., ed. 1984. *International Dimensions of Land Reform.* Boulder, Colo.: Westview Press.

Moore, Barrington, Jr. 1966. *Social Origins of Dictatorship and Democracy.* Boston: Beacon Press.

Moosbrugger, Bernhard, and Gladys Weigner. 1972. *A Voice of the Third World: Dom Helder Cámara.* New York: Pyramid Books.

Morawetz, David. 1977. *Twenty-Five Years of Economic Development, 1950 to 1975.* Baltimore: Johns Hopkins University Press.

Myrdal, G. 1957. *Economic Theory and Underdeveloped Regions.* London: Geral Duckworth.

Nolan, Peter. 1983. "De-collectivisation of Agriculture in China, 1979–82: A Long-Term Perspective." *Cambridge Journal of Economics* 7: 381–403.

O'Brien, Philip J. 1975. "A Critique of Latin American Theories of Dependency." In *Beyond the Sociology of Development*, ed. Ivar Oxaal, Tony Barnett, and David Booth. London: Routledge and Kegan Paul, 7–27.

Otero, Gerardo. 1989. "Agrarian Reform in Mexico: Capitalism and the State." In Thiesenhusen 1989d, 276–304.

Parsons, Kenneth H., R. J. Penn, and P. M. Raup. 1956. *Land Tenure: Proceedings of the International Conference on Land Tenure and Related Problems in World Agriculture Held at Madison, Wisconsin, 1951.* Madison: University of Wisconsin Press.

Patch, Richard W. 1965. "A Strategy of Anthropological Research in the Nation." *West Coast South America Series* (American Universities Field Staff) 12: 1–10.

Penn, Raymond J. 1961. "Public Interest in Private Property (Land)." *Land Economics* 37: 99–104.

Portes, Alejandro, Manuel Castells, and Lauren A. Benton, eds. 1989. *The Informal Economy.* Baltimore: Johns Hopkins University Press.

Powell, J. D. 1971. *Political Mobilization of the Venezuelan Peasant.* Cambridge, Mass.: Harvard University Press.

Powelson, John P., and Richard Stock. 1987. *The Peasant Betrayed: Agriculture and Land Reform in the Third World.* Boston: Lincoln Institute of Land Policy, Oelgeschlager, Gunn and Hain.

Prebisch, Raúl. 1950. *The Economic Development of Latin America and Its Principal Problems.* New York: United Nations.

Prebisch, Raúl. 1980. "Toward a Theory of Change." *CEPAL Review*, no. 9 (April): 155–208.

Prosterman, Roy L. 1972. "Land Reform as Foreign AID." *Foreign Policy* (Spring): 128–41.

Prosterman, Roy L., Jeffrey M. Riedinger, and Mary N. Temple. 1981. "Land Reform and the El Salvador Crisis." *International Security* 6 (Summer): 53–74.

Putterman, Louis. 1985. "The Restoration of the Peasant Household as Farm Production Unit in China: Some Incentive Theoretic Analyses." In *The Politi-*

cal Economy of Reform in Post-Mao China, ed. Elizabeth Perry and Christine Wong. Harvard Contemporary China Series. Cambridge, Mass.: Harvard University Press, 63–82.

Putterman, Louis. 1987. "The Incentive Problem and the Demise of Team Farming in China." *Journal of Development Economics* 26: 103–27.

Rao, C. H. 1975. *Technological Change and Distribution of Gains in Indian Agriculture*. New Delhi: Macmillan and Co..

Raup, Philip M. 1967. "Land Reform and Agricultural Development." In *Agricultural Development and Economic Growth*, ed. Herman M. Southworth and Bruce F. Johnston. Ithaca, N. Y.: Cornell University Press, 267–314.

Reed, Edward. 1977. "Introducing Group Farming in Less Developed Countries: Some Issues." In *Cooperative and Commune: Group Farming in the Economic Development of Agriculture*, ed. Peter Dorner. Madison: University of Wisconsin Press, 359–79.

Reed, Edward. 1978. "Organizational Issues in Group Farming in South Korea." LTC Paper, no. 119. Madison: Land Tenure Center, University of Wisconsin. December.

Reinhardt, Nola. 1989. "Contrast and Congruence in the Agrarian Reforms of El Salvador and Nicaragua." In Thiesenhusen 1989d, 451–82.

Saini, G. 1971. "Holding Size, Productivity and Some Related Aspects of Indian Agriculture." *Economic and Political Weekly*, 26 June 1971, A79–A84.

Salas, O., F. Knight, and C. Saenz. 1970. *Land Titling in Costa Rica: A Legal and Economic Survey*. San José: USAID/University of Costa Rica Law School. April.

Sazama, Geraldo, and Harlan L. Davis. 1973. "Land Taxation and Land Reform." *Economic Development and Cultural Change* 21, no. 4: 642–54.

Schuh, G. Edward. 1984. Comments on "The Political Economy of Rural Development in Latin America," by Alain de Janvry. In *Agricultural Development in the Third World*, ed. Carl K. Eicher and John M. Staatz. Baltimore: Johns Hopkins University Press, 96–109.

Schuh, G. Edward. 1989. "The Rationale for International Agricultural Education for the 21st Century." In *Educating for a Global Perspective: International Agricultural Curricula for 2005*. Madison: University of Wisconsin Press, 1–11.

Schweigert, Thomas. 1989. "Land Tenure Issues in Agricultural Development Projects in Latin America." LTC Paper, no. 132. Madison: Land Tenure Center, University of Wisconsin. April.

Sen, Abhijit. 1981. "Market Failure and Control of Labour Power; Towards an Explanation of Structure and Change in Indian Agriculture, Parts I and II." *Cambridge Journal of Economics* 5: 228–81, 327–50.

Sen, Chiranjib. 1983. Review of *Agrarian Crisis and Reformism in Latin America: A Review of the Agrarian Question and Reformism in Latin America*, by Alain de Janvry. *Economic and Political Weekly*, 24–31 December, A118–A120.

Shalom, Stephen R. 1977. "Counter-Insurgency in the Philippines." *Journal of Contemporary Asia* 7: 153–77.

104   References

Shearer, Eric B., Susana Lastarria-Cornhiel, and Dina Mesbah. 1990. "Rural Land Markets in Latin America and the Caribbean: Research, Theory, and Policy Implications." Madison: Land Tenure Center, University of Wisconsin. July.
Singer, H. W. 1950. "Trade and Investment in Underdeveloped Areas." *American Economic Review* 40 (May): 473–85.
Skocpol, Theda. 1982. "What Makes Peasants Revolutionary." *Comparative Politics* 14: 351–75.
Stanfield, J. David. 1985. "Projects That Title Land in Central and South America and the Caribbean: Expectations and Problems." LTC Paper, no. 126. Madison: Land Tenure Center, University of Wisconsin. June.
Stanfield, J. David. 1989. "Agrarian Reform in the Dominican Republic." In Thiesenhusen 1989d, 305–37.
Stavenhagen, Rodolfo. 1981. *Between Underdevelopment and Revolution.* New Delhi: Abhinav Publications.
Stewart, Stephen, Peter Fairhurst, and Guillermo Pedroni. 1987. "Evaluation of Commercial Land Market Project." Prepared for Agency for International Development Project, PIO/T No. 520-0000.1-3-70030. n.p.
Strasma, John. 1989. "Unfinished Business: Consolidating Land Reform in El Salvador." In Thiesenhusen 1989d, 408–28.
Strasma, John, James Alm, Eric Shearer, and Alfred Waldstein. 1987. "The Impact of Agricultural Land Revenue Systems on Agricultural Land Usage in Developing Countries." n.p. (Report to USAID.)
Stringer, Randy. 1989a. "Farmland Transfers and the Role of Land Banks in Latin America." LTC Paper, no. 131. Madison: Land Tenure Center, University of Wisconsin. April.
Stringer, Randy. 1989b. "Honduras: Toward Conflict and Agrarian Reform." In Thiesenhusen 1989d, 358–83.
Stringer, Randy, William C. Thiesenhusen, Patricia Ballard, and Wayne Kussow. 1985. "Institutional and Land Constraints to Irrigated Agriculture in the Azua Plains of the Dominican Republic." LTC Research Paper, no. 87. Madison: Land Tenure Center, University of Wisconsin. July.
Sunkel, Osvaldo. 1969. "National Development Policy and External Dependency in Latin America." *Journal of Development Studies* 6 (October): 23–48.
Sunkel, Osvaldo. 1971. "Capitalismo transnacional y desintegración nacional." *Trimestre Económico* (April-June): 571–628.
Sunkel, O., and P. Paz. 1973. *El subdesarrollo latinoamericano y la teoría del desarrollo.* Mexico: Siglo Veintiuno Editores.
Sunkel, O., and Edmundo F. Fuenzalida. 1979. "Transnationalization and Its National Consequences." In *Transnational Capitalism and National Development,* ed. J. J. Villamil. Atlantic Highlands, N.J.: Humanities Press, 67–93.
Thiesenhusen, William C. 1985. "National Security Implications of Land Reform in Third World Nations." *Oklahoma Law Review* 38: 789–98.
Thiesenhusen, William C. 1989a. "Blaming the Victim: Latin American Agricultural Land Tenure System and the Environmental Debate." Madison: Land Tenure Center. October.

Thiesenhusen, William C. 1989b. "Conclusions: Searching for Agrarian Reform in Latin America." In Thiesenhusen 1989d, 483–503.

Thiesenhusen, William C. 1989c. "Introduction: Searching for Agrarian Reform in Latin America." In Thiesenhusen 1989d, 1–41.

Thiesenhusen, William C. 1991. "Implications of the Rural Land Tenure System for the Environmental Debate: Three Scenarios." *Journal of Developing Areas* (forthcoming).

Thiesenhusen, William C., ed. 1989d. *Searching for Agrarian Reform in Latin America*. Boston: Unwin Hyman.

Thiesenhusen, William C., and Jolyne Melmed-Sanjak. 1990. "Brazil's Agrarian Structure: Changes from 1970 through 1980." *World Development* 18: 393–415.

Thome, Joseph R. 1989. "Law, Conflict, and Change: Frei's Law and Allende's Agrarian Reform." In Thiesenhusen 1989d, 188–215.

United States. 1985. "International Security and Development Cooperation Act of 1985." Section 1208 (Public Law 99-83, 99 Statute 277). *Statutes at Large*.

Vekemans, S. J., Roger E. 1964. "Economic Development, Social Change, and Cultural Mutation in Latin America." In *Religion, Revolution, and Reform*, edited by William V. D'Antonio and Fredrick B. Pike. New York: Praeger, 129–42.

Venezuela. Ministerio de Agricultura y Cría. 1979. *Agrarian Reform and Rural Development in Venezuela*. World Conference on Agrarian Reform and Rural Development. Rome: Food and Agriculture Organization.

Webb, R. 1975. "The Urban Traditional Sector in Peru." Mimeograph. Washington, D.C.: International Bank for Reconstruction and Development.

West, H. W. 1972. "Land Registration and Land Records: Their Role in Development." *Land and Water Economics and Policies*. A/D/C Teaching Forum, no. 1-rev. April. New York: Agricultural Development Council, 1–8.

White, Robert. 1985. "Aiding Contras Harms Democracy." *Christian Science Monitor*, 23 April.

World Bank. 1975. *Assault on World Poverty*. Baltimore: Johns Hopkins University Press.

World Bank. 1978. "Land Reform in Latin America: Bolivia, Chile, Mexico, Peru and Venezuela." World Bank, Staff Working Paper, no. 275. Washington, D.C.: World Bank.

World Bank. 1988. *World Development Report 1988*. New York: Oxford University Press.

Zevallos L., José Vicente. 1989. "Agrarian Reform and Structural Change: Ecuador since 1964." In Thiesenhusen 1989d, 42–69.

Zoomers, E. B. 1988. *Rural Development and Survival Strategies in Central Paraguay*. The Centre for Latin American Research and Documentation (CEDLA). The Netherlands: Foris Publications.

Index

Agrarian system: transformation of, 4–5
Agricultural collectivism: levels of integration, 55–56. *See also* Collective agriculture; Production cooperatives
Agricultural output structures: in Latin America, 63
Alliance for Progress: defining agenda of, 11, 32
American Civil War: slavery issue and land conflicts, 3
Argentina, 62
Australia: land taxation, 80

Bangladesh: financing land purchases, 65
Bolivia: twentieth-century revolution, 3; land reforms, 32, 49–50; mentioned, 5, 51, 62
Brazil: farm size and factor productivities, 26–27; land reforms, 48–49; international comparisons, 61; land taxation, 80; land financing, 81, 83; mentioned, 62, 65

Caribbean: land reforms, 41–42
Catholic Church: role in land reforms, 19–21
Central America: land financing experiments, 80–82
Chile: reform legislation, 33; land reforms, 38–39; reorganization of *asentamientos*, 52; mentioned, 7, 62, 79
China: Communist revolution, 32; decollectivization, 53; mentioned, 5
Cold War, 32. *See also* East-West conflicts
Collective agriculture: problems with, 53–55. *See also* Agricultural collectivism; Production cooperatives
Colombia: farm size and productivity, 26; land reforms, 46; land taxation, 79; mentioned, 62
Colonialism: internal, 17
Costa Rica: colonization, 33; land titling,

77; land financing, 82, 90; mentioned, 62, 65
Cuba: revolution, 11, 32; mentioned, 3, 5, 7, 34, 52

Decolonization, 14
Dominican Republic: land reforms, 40–41; privatization of production cooperatives, 52–53; mentioned, 33, 51, 54

Eastern Europe, 53, 92
East-West conflicts: and Third World reforms, 7–8. *See also* Cold War
Economic Commission for Latin America, 16
Ecuador: land reforms, 35–37, 63; land financing, 81, 82, 83; mentioned, 33, 62, 65
Egypt, 32
El Salvador: land reforms, 44–46; land titling, 77–78; mentioned, 3, 51, 52
Environmental protection: and tenure systems, 68; recognized by international banks, 68–69
Ethiopia, 5

Feudal relations, 9, 21, 22
Fondo Ecuatoriano Popularum Progressio, 83
Free trade and development, 15
French Revolution: and peasant rights, 3
Fulbright, William: reform and U.S. policy, 8

Gini coefficients, 70
Green Revolution: and the inverse relation, 23–26 *passim*
Guatemala: land redistribution, 32; land financing, 81–82

Homestead Act of 1862, U.S., 3
Honduras: land reforms, 43; off-farm incomes, 64; mentioned, 51, 52, 62, 81